FOLLOWING CHRIST

Losing Your Life for His Sake

CHARLES H. SPURGEON

ANEKO
PRESS

We love hearing from our readers. Please contact us
at www.anekopress.com/questions-comments with
any questions, comments, or suggestions.

Printed in the United States of America

Aneko Press

www.anekopress.com

Aneko Press, Life Sentence Publishing, and our logos are trademarks of

Life Sentence Publishing, Inc.
203 E. Birch Street
P.O. Box 652
Abbotsford, WI 54405

RELIGION / Christian Ministry / General

Paperback ISBN: 978-1-62245-605-5
eBook ISBN: 978-1-62245-606-2

10 9 8 7 6 5 4 3 2 1

Available where books are sold

Contents

Chapter 1

The Necessity of Following Christ

Follow me, and I will make you fishers of men.
(Matthew 4:19)

Y ou cannot have Christ if you will not serve Him. If you
take Christ, you must take Him in all His qualities. You
must not simply take Him as a Friend, but you must also take
Him as your Master. If you are to become His disciple, you
must also become His servant. I hope that no one fights against
that truth. It is certainly one of our greatest delights on earth
to serve our Lord, and this is to be our joyful vocation even in
heaven itself: *His servants shall serve Him: and they shall see
His face* (Revelation 22:3-4).

This thought also enters into our idea of salvation. To be
saved means that we are rescued from the slavery of sin and
brought into the delightful liberty of the servants of God. We
can sincerely pray: "O Master, You are such a glorious Lord that
serving You is perfect freedom and sweetest rest! You have told
us that it would be so, and we have found it so."

*Take my yoke upon you, and learn of me; for I am meek and
lowly in heart: and ye shall find rest unto your souls* (Matthew
11:29). We do find this to be true. It is not as though rest were a

separate thing from service, for the very service itself becomes rest to our souls. I do not know how some of us would have any rest on earth if we could not live our daily lives in the service of Christ. The *rest* that we see in heaven is never to be pictured as idleness or boredom, but as constantly being permitted to have the high privilege of serving the Lord.

Learn from this, then, all of you who would like to have Christ as your Savior, that you must be willing to serve Him. We are not saved *by* serving Him, but we are saved *to* serve Him. From the moment we are saved, we ought to live in the service of our Lord. If we refuse to be His servants, we are not saved, for we evidently still remain the servants of self and the servants of Satan.

> **We are not saved *by* serving Him, but we are saved *to* serve Him.**

Holiness is another name for salvation. To be delivered from the power of self-will, the domination of evil lusts, and the tyranny of Satan – this is salvation. Those who desire to be saved must know that they will have to serve Christ. Those who are really saved rejoice that they are serving Him, and they are giving evidence of a changed heart and a renewed mind.

So are you proposing to yourself that you will serve Christ? You are a young man. You have plenty of vigor and strength, and you say to yourself, "I will serve Christ in some remarkable way. I will try to make myself a scholar, I will try to learn the art of public speaking, and I will in some way or other glorify my Lord's name by the magnificence of my speech."

Will you, dear friend? Is it not better, if you are going to serve Christ, to ask Him what He would like you to do? If you wanted to do something kind for a friend, you would certainly want to know what would best please that friend, or else your kindness might be mistaken, and you might be doing that which would cause difficulty rather than help. Listen to me. Your Lord and

Master does not require you to become either a scholar or an orator in order to serve Him. You might become both of those things in your career, but first of all He says, *If any man serve me, let him follow me* (John 12:26).

More than anything else, Jesus desires that His servants would follow Him. If we do that, we will serve Him in the way that is according to His own choice. I notice that many good friends want to serve Christ by standing on the top rung of the ladder. You cannot get there all in one step, young man.

A better way would be to serve Christ by following Him, by doing the next thing you can do, that simple little thing that you are able to do that will bring you no special honor, but which, nevertheless, is what your Lord desires from you. In effect, you can hear Him say to you, "If anyone desires to serve Me, let him follow Me, not by aiming at great things, but by just doing that work that I put before him at the time." *Seekest thou great things for thyself?* said the prophet Jeremiah to Baruch. *Seek them not* (Jeremiah 45:5). I say the same thing to you.

One friend might be blessed with great riches and say, "I will keep getting more until I acquire a very large amount, and then I will build apartments for the poor, will give a lot of money to some new foreign missionary effort, or I will build a large church in which Christ's name will be preached." God forbid that I would stop you from doing something good, but if you want to do what is absolutely certain to please Christ, I would not recommend the selection of any one particular object, but I would advise you just to do this: follow Him, remembering that He said, *If any man serve me, let him follow me.*

If you simply walk behind your Master, following His footsteps and truly being His disciple, you will do what pleases Him more than if you could donate to His cause with a whole pile of riches. This is what He selects as the best proof of your love and the best testimony of your regard for Him: *If any man serve me, let him follow me.* He requires of you that you become as a little child so that you may be taught by Him. His own words are, *Except ye be converted, and become as little children, ye shall not enter into the kingdom of heaven* (Matthew 18:3). If you want to be a servant of Christ, come to Him as a little child; sit down before Him and let Him teach you the basic principles of the gospel.

If any man serve me, let him follow me. "You must follow Me as My disciple, regarding Me as your teacher, to whom you bow your understanding and your entire mind so that I may form them according to My own will." This is the language of our Lord, and I want to impress it very firmly upon you all, and especially upon any who are beginning the Christian life. If you intend to serve Jesus, make your mind like a tablet of wax under His stylus, that He may write on you whatsoever He pleases. Be Christ's slate, that He may make His mark on you. Be His sheet of paper on which He may write His living letters of love. You can serve Him in this way in the best possible manner.

Whatsoever He saith unto you, do it (John 2:5). If you really want to serve Christ, do not do what you suggest to yourself, but do what He commands you. Remember what Samuel said to Saul: *To obey is better than sacrifice, and to hearken than the fat of rams* (1 Samuel 15:22). I believe that the profession of consecration to God, when it is accompanied by action that I suggest to myself, may be nothing but worship of the will, an abomination in the sight of God; but when anyone says to the Lord, "What do You want me to do? Show me, my Master, what You have for me to do," – when there is a real desire to obey every command of Christ, then there is the true spirit of service and the true spirit of sonship.

"If anyone wants to serve Me, let him follow Me, running at My call, following at My heels, waiting at My feet to do whatsoever I desire him to do." This makes life much simpler than some imagine it to be. You are not to go and carve a statue out of marble by the exercise of your own genius; if that were the task set before us, most of us would never accomplish it. You only have to go and write according to Christ's own example, to copy His letters, the upstrokes and the downstrokes, and to write exactly as He has written.

The other day, I was asked to sign my name to a deed, and when it was handed to me, I said, "I have already signed my name!"

"Yes," said the one who brought it, "you have the very easy job of writing it all over again." In that case, I simply traced my own writing; and you have the easy task of writing after Christ, tracing over again the letters that He Himself has made, and you cannot serve Him any better than this. Jesus says, "If anyone wants to serve Me, let him follow Me. Let him do just what I ask him to do. Follow Me by imitating My example."

It is always safe to do what Jesus would have done under the same circumstances in which you are placed. Of course, you cannot imitate Him in His miraculous work, and you are not asked to imitate Him in some of those sorrowful respects in which He suffered so that we would not suffer, but the ordinary life of Christ is in every respect an example to us. Never do what you could not suppose Jesus would have done.

If it occurs to you that the course of action that is suggested to you would be un-Christlike, then it is un-Christian, for the Christian is to be like Christ. The Christian is to be the flower growing out of Christ, the seed; and there is always a right attachment between the flower and the seed out of which it grows. Keep your eyes fixed on your heavenly example and pattern, and seek in all things to always imitate Jesus. If you want to serve Christ, repeat His life as nearly as possible in your own life. "If anyone wants to serve Me, let him follow Me by copying My example."

You do not need to run away from your father and mother, leave your home and friends, and go away to Africa in order to serve Jesus. It is not getting some superficial idea in your own mind and carrying it out according to your own notions and thoughts that constitutes service for Christ. It is just simply this: If anyone will serve Christ, let him follow Christ. Let him put his foot down as nearly as he can where Christ put His foot down. Let him tread in Christ's steps and be moved by His principles. Let him be motivated by His motives, live with His purposes, and copy His actions. This is the noblest way in which to serve the Lord.

If any man serve me, let him follow me; and where I am, there shall also my servant be (John 12:26). I do not know any other master except Jesus Christ who ever said that. There are some places where an earthly master does not want his servant to be. He must have some time to himself. He has some things to do that he cannot explain to his servant. He has some matters into which his servant must not pry. But the Lord Jesus Christ makes the glorious privilege of everyone who enters His service that where He is, there His servant will be also.

If you want to walk with God, then you must walk!

But where is Christ? He is and always was in the place of communion with God. He was always near to His Father. He often spoke with God. He always had the joy of God filling His spirit. Perhaps you are saying to yourself, "I wish that I had communion with God." Well, through Jesus Christ, it can be had by serving Him in that particular kind of service that consists in following Him.

If you want to walk with God, then you must walk! If you sit down in idleness, you cannot walk with Him. If you do not keep up a good brisk pace, He will walk on in front of you and leave you behind, for the Lord is no straggler in His walking. Therefore, you see, there must be diligent progress and activity in serving Him in order that we may keep pace with Him and have communion with Him. If we live like this here, He has promised that we will be in the place of communion with our blessed Master.

Our Lord Jesus Christ went about His work with confidence. Whenever Christ went to work, He worked with assurance. He never had a doubt as to His ultimate success. No haphazard work ever came from His hands. He spoke with certainty, and He worked with the full assurance that His labor would not be in vain. If you want to have confidence in your work for Christ so as to perform it without any doubts and fears, you will have to obtain it by serving Him, and to serve Him by following Him; then you, too, will arrive in that hallowed place of confidence where your Master always stood.

It is very sweet to notice how the Lord Jesus brings His Father into His speech; it is as if He said, "When a person joins himself to Me, he joins himself to My Father also. It is not only I who will love him and will do My best to honor him, but My Father, the great and ever-blessed Lord over all, keeps an eye on that person." On whom does He look with this gaze of approval? Not on those who have some big intention of serving themselves, but on those who serve Christ and who do it by following Him.

It is delightful to have a sense of the approval of God, such as you never had when you had the approval of people. Sometimes, when even Christian people cry, "Well done, well done," the Lord says, "That is quite enough praise for him; I will not give him My 'Well done.'" But when you get no "Well done" from men, but on the contrary, are misunderstood and misrepresented, then the Lord comes and puts His hand upon you, and says, "Be strong, fear not, for I have accepted your service. I know your motive, and I approve your action. Do not be afraid of them, but go on your way." Such approval as that is the highest honor we can have here. *If any man serve me, him will my Father honour* (John 12:26), Jesus said, with a sense of sonship and with a sense of approval.

If anyone will serve Christ by following Him, the Father will give him honor in the eyes of the blood-bought family. There are certain of the Lord's people who do not carry tape measures with them, but they carry scales and weights, and they do not measure by quantity, but they measure by quality; their approval is worth having. They are often the poorest and most afflicted members of the church, but being the most instructed and living the nearest to God, to be held in honor by them is a thing worth having.

I believe that if anyone will live the life of a Christian, however few his talents, and if his service lies in close obedience to Christ and imitation of Christ, the real saints, not merely those who profess to be Christians, and especially not the worldly ones among them, but real saints will say, "That is the man for us; that is the woman we like to be around and have discussions with and pray with." Those who really do serve the Lord by following Him are held in honor by those who fellowship with them at their Lord's table.

Then, when we come to die, or when we stand at the judgment seat of Christ, or when we enter upon the eternal state, what a glorious thing it will be to find the Father ready to honor us forever because we served the Son! Our reward will not be of debt, but of grace (Romans 4:4). It is grace that gave us the ability to serve Him, and it is grace that will reward us for our service. No man or woman will serve the Lord Jesus Christ here on earth by following Him without finding that the Father has some special honor, some rich and rare reward, to give to such soldiers in due time.

This is the day of battle. Expect nothing now but bullets, bruises, wounds, and scars; but the battle will soon be over, and when the war is ended, the King will come and ride up and down the ranks, and in that day you who have been most battered and most wounded in the battle will see Him stop when He reaches you, and He will fasten on you a star that will be more honor to you than all the Medals of Honor that have decorated brave men here below. Earthly rewards and honors are for those who want them, but blessed are they who shall shine as the stars in the kingdom of our Father! This honor is to be obtained by that believer who will faithfully serve his Lord, and not by any who merely talk about it, dream of it, or intend to do it. This honor will be given to those who serve Jesus by following Him.

Chapter 2

How to Go

And they went forth, and preached every where, the
Lord working with them. (Mark 16:20)

I like the thought of Christ being taken up to heaven because His work was done, and His people being left on earth because there was still work for them to do. If we could leave this earth for heaven, what a pity it would be if we should do so while there is a single soul to be saved! I think that if I had not brought to Christ the full number of jewels that He intended me to bring to adorn His crown, I would ask to come back again, even from heaven. He knows best where we can best serve Him, so He ordains that, while He sits at the right hand of God, we are to abide here and go forth to preach everywhere, the Lord working with us.

The disciples worked **aggressively**. They went forth. Some of them needed to stay for a while at Jerusalem, though that old nest was eventually pulled down. Not a stick of it was left, and the very tree on which it was built was cut down. Persecution drove most of them farther and farther away from Jerusalem. We do not know where they all went. There are traditions, which are not very valuable, to show where each of the apostles went, but it is quite certain that they all went somewhere or other. Starting from the one common center, they went in various directions preaching Christ. They worked. They went forth and preached.

The disciples did not say, "Well, the Master has gone to heaven, the eternal purposes of God will be quite sure to be carried out, and it is not possible that the designs of infinite love should fail, especially as He is at the Father's side; therefore, let us enjoy ourselves spiritually. Let us sit down in the happy possession of covenant blessings and sing to our hearts' content because of all that God has done for us and given to us. He will bring about His own purposes, and we only have to stand still and see the salvation of God."

No, it was not for them to judge what they should do. When they were told to remain at Jerusalem, they remained at Jerusalem. There are times of waiting, but inasmuch as the Master had commanded them to go into all the world and preach the gospel to every creature, they also, when the time had come, went into all the world and began to preach everywhere the gospel they had learned at Jesus' feet.

It is not for us to judge what would seem most reasonable, much less what would be most comfortable. Our duty is to do as we are instructed, when we are directed to do so, and because we are ordered to do so, for we are servants and not masters. It is not wise to plan out the proceedings even of a single day on our own, but to take our direction from Him who is our guide and leader, and to follow Him in all things.

There are some who do not attend church all the time because they are at work for Christ in some way or other. They are at work in some mission station, or trying to open a new room for preaching, or doing something else for the Master; the Lord bless them! I do not want all of the people to go out at the same time, but I do want you all to know that while it may be the beginning, it is not the end or the peak of the Christian life to come and hear sermons.

Scatter the blessing of God's truth as widely as you can. The moment you find the light and realize that the world is in the dark, take your light and share it with someone else. Be glad that you have the light yourself, but if God gives you a candle and all you do is lock yourself up in a room, sit down, and say, "Sweet light! sweet light! I have got the light while all the world is in the dark; sweet, sweet light!" your candle will soon burn out, and you also will be

> We must seek to bring sinners to Jesus whether we offend people or whether we please them.

in the dark. However, if you go to others and say, "I will have just as much light if I give some to you," by this means God the Holy Spirit will pour upon you fresh beams of light, and you will shine brighter and brighter, even to the perfect day.

They went forth. I wish some people I know of could have their safe little chapels burned down! They have remained out of the way down a side street for the last hundred years. They are good souls, and they should be. They should be mature by now after so much time inside; but if they would only come out in the street, they might do much more good than they are currently doing.

"Oh, but there is an old deacon who does not like street preaching!" I know him very well; he will be gone to heaven soon. Then, as soon as you have had his funeral sermon, get out into the street and begin somehow or other to make Christ known. Oh, to break down every barrier and get rid of every restraint that hides the blessed gospel! Perhaps we must respect these dear old believers' feelings just a little, but not so much as to let souls die; we must seek to bring sinners to Jesus whether we offend people or whether we please them.

These disciples went forth **promptly**, for though there is not a word here about the time, it is implied that as soon as the hour had struck and the Holy Spirit had descended from Christ and rested upon them, they went forth and preached the word everywhere. Sadly, far too often we are "going" to do something! If we did about a tenth part of what we say we are going to do, much more might be accomplished! *They went forth*. They did not talk about going forth, but they went forth. They did not wait until they received directions from the apostles where they were to go, but the Lord guided each man, and each man went his own way, preaching the gospel of Jesus Christ.

You believe the gospel, and you believe that people are perishing for lack of it; therefore, I urge you, do not stop to consider and do not wait to contemplate any longer. The best way to spread the gospel is to preach the gospel. I believe the best way of defending the gospel is to spread the gospel.

They served their Master **obediently**. They went forth and preached. Suppose they had gone forth and had a music concert! Suppose they had gone forth and held a meeting that was partly fun and entertaining, with just a little bit of a moral story added to the end of it! We would have been in the darkness of paganism to the present day. There is nothing that is really of any service for the preaching of the gospel except preaching.

By preaching, I mean, as I have already said, not just standing up in the pulpit and delivering a speech, but talking about Christ – talking about Him as risen from the dead, as the judge of the living and the dead, as the great atoning sacrifice, the one mediator between God and men. It is by preaching Jesus Christ that sinners are saved. *It pleased God by the foolishness of preaching to save them that believe* (1 Corinthians 1:21).

Whatever may be said outside the Bible about preaching, you only have to turn to the Word of God itself to find what a divine ordinance it is and to see how the Lord makes that to be the primary means of our salvation. This is the gun that will win the battle yet, though many have tried to silence it. They have had all sorts of new inventions and strategies, but when all their inventions will have had their day and proved futile, you can be sure that the proclaiming of Jesus Christ's name, gospel, and work among mankind will be effective when everything else will have failed.

They went forth and preached. It is not said that they went forth and argued, or that they went forth and wrote apologetics manuals for the Christian faith. No, they went forth and proclaimed God's Word. They spoke out the truth as a revelation from God. In the name of Jesus Christ, they demanded that people should believe in Him, and they left them, if they would not believe, with the distinct understanding that they would perish in their unbelief. They wept over them and pleaded with them to believe in Jesus. They were certain that whosoever did believe in Him would find eternal life through His name. This is what the whole church of Christ should do, and do at once, and keep on doing with all its might, even until the end of the age.

There is one more word – **everywhere**. One of our great writers, in a very amusing letter that he wrote to someone who had asked for a contribution towards the removal of a chapel debt, asked why we cannot preach Christ behind hedges and in ditches – in the fields instead of in church buildings. Of course we can preach outdoors, and we must do so, provided it does not rain too hard. Can we not preach Jesus Christ at a street corner? Of course we can; yet in such a climate as ours, we often need buildings in which we can worship God, but we must never get into the idea of confining our preaching to the building.

They went forth and preached everywhere. Some people complained about John Wesley for not confining his preaching to the area of his church, or his parish. Wesley insisted that he did, for he said that all the world was his parish; and all the world is every man's parish. Do good everywhere, wherever you may be. Some of you are going to the ocean for a vacation; do not go without a lot of gospel tracts, and do not go without seeking an opportunity, when you are sitting on the beach, to talk to people about the Lord Jesus Christ.

A man I knew had nothing particular to do except to go and sit down on a seat in Hyde Park and talk there with men and women who came and sat there. He

Is it not gracious and kind on the Lord's part to let us come and work with Him?

would tell them that he had a pew at the Tabernacle,[1] and he would lend them his ticket so that they might have a comfortable place; then he took care after the sermon to talk to them about Christ. He said, "I myself cannot preach, but I can bring people to hear my minister, and I can ask God to bless them when they come."

I saw another brother who leaves his home at 8:00 a.m. every Sunday. There are, or there were, church members who walked twelve miles every Sunday morning to hear the gospel, and then walked back again to their homes at night. This brother starts at 8:00 a.m. and puts one of my sermons into each of the mailboxes in a certain district as he walks along[2]. So he takes advantage of his long walk, and in the course of the year circulates many thousand sermons. What an excellent way he has found of spending the Sunday morning! Having done that service for his Lord, he enjoys the gospel all the better because of what he has himself done in making it known to others.

You remember the passage in which we are said to be *labourers together with God* (1 Corinthians 3:9). Is it not gracious and

---

1 The Metropolitan Tabernacle was the church in London where Spurgeon preached. Members could rent a pew and were given tickets to use for that pew. People could also attend the Metropolitan Tabernacle without having a ticket, of course.

2 Publisher's Note: In the United States, it is not legal to put anything in other individuals' mailboxes and we'd suggest finding an alternative location to leave evangelistic materials.

kind on the Lord's part to let us come and work with Him? Yet it seems to my mind even more gracious for God to come and work with us, because ours is such poor, feeble, imperfect service, yet He does so – *the Lord working with them* (Mark 16:20). The Lord is working with that dear sister who, when she teaches her Sunday school class, feels that she is quite unfit for it. He is working with that brother who, when he preaches, thinks that he has not preached at all and is half-inclined never to try again. Oh, yes, *the Lord working with them*, such as they were, – fishermen, humble women, and the like! This is wonderful how God reaches down to us!

The Holy Spirit took what they said and made it to be divinely powerful. However feebly they uttered it according to the judgment of men, there was an inward secret power that went with their utterances and compelled the hearts of men and women to accept the blessed appeal of God. I believe that when we are seeking to serve Christ, we do not often know how very wonderfully God is working with us.

I have an example. There was a certain district of which I heard that there was much need of the gospel, and that there were many people in that district who were as ignorant of the way of salvation as those who had never heard of the Bible. The various churches seemed to affect only a very small proportion of the people. A brother visited the neighborhood for me, and I prayed very earnestly that his visits might be blessed. It is a very interesting thing that while I was thinking about that district, there were certain Christian people close to it who were thinking about me and longing for the gospel to be carried to their neighbors.

After I had thought of this matter only a little, I received a letter from them saying how much they wanted somebody to come and labor for the Lord among them. I said to myself, "This is strange. I have known this district for years, yet I have never noticed that anybody wanted me or my message; but the moment I begin to move towards the people, they begin to move towards me." You do not know that you may not have a similar story to tell. There is that street you feel moved to go and work in; God has been there ahead of you. Do you not remember how, when His children had to go and destroy the Canaanites, the Lord sent the hornet before them? *I sent hornets before you, which drove them out from before you* (Joshua 24:12). Now, when you have to go and preach to sinners, God sends some preparatory work before you; He is sure to do so.

In other cases, God works afterward. Sometimes it is immediately afterward, and at other times, it is years later. There are different sorts of seeds in the world. The seeds of some plants and trees, unless they undergo a peculiar process, will not grow for years. There is something about them that preserves them intact for a long time, but in due season the life germ shoots forth. In the same way, there are certain kinds of people who do not catch the truth at the time it is uttered, and it lies hidden away in their souls until one day, under peculiar circumstances, they remember what they heard, and it begins to affect their hearts.

If we work and God works with us, what is there that we may not expect? Therefore, the great need of any Christian worker is for God to work with him, and therefore, it ought to be our daily confession that we need God to work with us. We must always realize that we are nothing apart from His working. We must not pretend to praise the Holy Spirit by every once in a while talking about Him, as though it were the right thing to say that of course the Holy Spirit must work. It must be an absolute matter of fact with us that the Holy Spirit must work, as much as it would be with a miller that his sails could not go around without the wind;[3] and then we must act as the

---

3   This is referring to a miller, one who mills grain, and the sails, or blades, on his windmill.

miller does. He sets his sails and tries to catch the wind from whatever direction it blows, and we must try to work in such a way that the Holy Spirit is likely to bless us.

I do not think the Holy Spirit will bless just any act of service that is done even by well-meaning people, because if He did, it would seem as if He had set His seal to a great deal that was not according to the mind of the Lord. Let us so act in our work that there is never even the smudge of a dirty thumb across the page, and nothing of pride, self-seeking, or anger. Instead, let all that we do be done in humility, in dependence upon God, and in faith – and always in a holy and gracious spirit, so that we can expect the Holy Spirit to take it over and bless it. That will, of course, involve that everything must be done prayerfully, for our Heavenly Father gives the Holy Spirit to those who ask Him (Luke 11:13); and we must ask for this greatest of blessings, that God the Holy Spirit may work with our work.

Then we must believe in the Holy Spirit, and believe to the highest degree, so as never to be discouraged or think anything is too difficult. *Is any thing too hard for the Lord?* (Genesis 18:14). Can anything be difficult for the Holy Spirit? It is often an imposing thing to get into deep water so as to be forced to swim, as we like to keep our feet touching the sand. What mercy it is to feel that you cannot do anything, for then you must trust in God and God alone, believing that He is quite equal to any emergency! Thus trusting and doing His will, we will not fail. Come, Holy Spirit, and work with all Your people now! Come and stir us up to work, and when we are stirred up with holy energy, then work with us!

Chapter 3

The Help of the Holy Spirit

*But the Comforter, which is the Holy Spirit, whom
the Father will send in my name, he shall teach you
all things and bring to your remembrance all the
things that I have said unto you.* (John 14:26)

Have faith in God, and never let your discovery of your
own weakness shake your firm conviction that *with
God all things are possible* (Matthew 19:26). It seems to me to
be a fountain of comfort and a storehouse of strength. Do not
limit the Holy One of Israel, nor conceive of the Holy Spirit
as confined and hindered by the difficulties that come up in
fallen human nature. No situation that you bring to Him with
affectionate tears and with an earnest faith in Jesus will ever
be dismissed as incurable. You never need to lose hope, for the
Lord of hosts is with us.

Sometimes we are troubled because of the hardness of people's hearts. You who work for the Lord know the most about
this. If anyone thinks that he can change a heart by his own
power, let him try with anyone he wants, and he will soon be at

a loss. "Old Adam is too strong for young Melanchthon."[4] Our trembling arm cannot roll away the stone of natural depravity.

Well, what then? The Spirit of the Lord is not straitened, or limited. *Is the spirit of the Lord straitened? are these his doings?* (Micah 2:7). Did I hear you cry, "Alas! I have tried to help an alcoholic recover, but he has gone back to his alcohol"? Yes, he has beaten *you,* but is the Spirit of the Lord inadequate?

Do you cry, "But he signed the pledge to abstain from alcohol, and yet he broke it"? Very likely *your* bonds are broken; but is the Spirit of the Lord confined? Can He not renew the heart and cast out the love of sin? When the Spirit of God works along with your help, your convert will keep his promise.

"Alas!" cries another, "I hoped I had rescued a woman involved in prostitution, but she has returned to her iniquity." This is not an unusual thing with those who are involved in that sin, but is the Spirit of the Lord restrained? Cannot He save the woman who was a sinner? Cannot He create a surpassing love to Jesus in her forgiven spirit?

We are baffled, but the Spirit is not. What narrow and shallow vessels we are! How soon we are empty! We wake up on Sunday morning and wonder where we will find strength for the day. Do you not sigh, "I do not think I can teach my Sunday school class today with any hope of teaching with power; I am so dreadfully downcast and disheartened; I feel scatterbrained and I have little thought and feeling"? In such a case ask yourself, *Is the Spirit of the Lord straitened?* He will help you. You want to speak to someone about his soul, but you fear that the right words will not come. You forget that He has promised to give you what you shall speak. "Is the Spirit of the Lord insufficient?" Cannot He prepare your heart and tongue?

No, the Spirit of the Lord is not limited. That promise is still

---

4   This is said to be the answer given by Martin Luther's friend and fellow reformer, Philipp Melanchthon (1497-1560), after Melanchthon had tried to preach God's truth in the power of the flesh.

our delight, *My grace is sufficient for thee* (2 Corinthians 12:9). It is a joy to become weak that we may say with the apostle, *When I am weak, then am I strong* (2 Corinthians 12:10). Behold, the strength of the Lord is gloriously revealed to perfection in our weakness. Come, you feeble workers, you fainting laborers, come and rejoice in the unlimited Spirit. Come, you who seem to plow the rock and till the sand, come and lay hold of the fact that the Spirit of the Lord is omnipotent. No rock will remain unbroken when He swings the hammer; no metal will be hard when He is the fire. Our Lord will still put His Spirit within us and clothe us with His power according to His promise, *As thy days, so shall thy strength be* (Deuteronomy 33:25).

> If there are no conversions, we cannot fall back upon the Spirit of God and blame Him.

Some people have said, "Yes, but then, see how few the conversions are nowadays! Many churches are poorly attended, and we have others where there are hardly any conversions from the beginning of the year to the end of it." This is all undeniable, and it is admitted with great regret; but is the Spirit of the Lord restrained? *Are these his doings?* (Micah 2:7).

Cannot we find some other reason much closer to the truth? If there are no conversions, we cannot fall back upon the Spirit of God and blame Him. Has Christ been preached? Has faith been exercised? The preacher must take his share of the blame; the church with which he is connected must also inquire whether there has been that degree of prayer for a blessing on the Word that there ought to have been. Christians must begin to look into their own hearts to find the reason for defeat.

If the work of God is hindered in our midst, there might be some secret sin within us that hinders the operation of the Spirit of God. God might be compelled by the very holiness of His character to refuse to work with an unholy or an unbelieving people. Have you never read, *He did not many mighty works there because of their unbelief* (Matthew 13:58)? Unbelief might be turning a fruitful land into barrenness. The Spirit Himself is not limited in His power, but our sin has made Him hide Himself from us. The lack of conversions cannot be blamed on Him. We have not gone forth in His strength. We shake off with disgust the smallest thought that would lay any blame to the Spirit of the Most High. Unto us be shame and confusion of face, as at this day (see Daniel 9:7).

It is also said that there is a general lack of power shown by individual Christians. Where are the men today like Elijah who can go up to the top of Mount Carmel and cover the heavens with clouds? Where are the apostolic men who convert nations? Where are the heroes and martyr spirits of the better days? Have we not fallen upon an age of insignificant men who dare little and do little? It may be so, but this is no fault of the great Spirit of God. Our degeneracy cannot be blamed on Him. We have destroyed ourselves, and only in Him is our help found. Instead of crying today, *Awake, awake . . . O arm of the Lord* (Isaiah 51:9), we ought to listen to the cry from heaven that says, *Awake, awake: put on thy strength, O Zion; put on thy beautiful garments. . . . Shake thyself from the dust* (Isaiah 52:1-2).

> Many of us might have accomplished great things for the Lord if we had but given our hearts to it.

Many of us might have accomplished great things for the Lord if we had but given our hearts to it. The weakest of us might have rivaled David, and the strongest among us might have been as angels of God. We are hindered because of ourselves; we have not reached out to the possibilities of strength that lie within our grasp. Let us not wickedly suggest that the good Spirit of our God is at fault, but let us in truthful humility blame ourselves. If we have not lived in the light, can we be surprised that we are mostly in the dark? If we have not fed upon the bread of heaven, should we be amazed that we are weak? Let us return unto the Lord. Let us seek again to be baptized into the Holy Spirit and into fire, and we will yet again behold the wonderful works of the Lord. He sets before us an open door, and if we do not enter, we have only ourselves to blame. He *giveth to all men liberally, and upbraideth not* (James 1:5), and if we still lack, we have not because we do not ask, or because we ask in a wrong manner. *Ye have not, because ye ask not. Ye ask, and receive not, because ye ask amiss* (James 4:2-3).

Look at the condition of the world. After the gospel has been in it over two thousand years, see how small a part of it is converted, how many cling to their idols, how much sin, error, poverty, and misery are still in the world! We know all these sad facts, but is this the fault of God's Holy Spirit? Tell me, when has the Holy Spirit created darkness or sin? Where has He been the author of vice or oppression? *Where do the wars and disputes come from?* (James 4:1). Do they come from Him? Do they not rather come from our own lusts?

What if the world was still an Augean stable, greatly needing cleansing?[5] Has the Spirit of God in any degree or sense made it so? Where the gospel has been fully preached, have not the words of the Lord done good to those who walk uprightly? Have not cannibals been redeemed and civilized? Has not the slave trade and other wickedness been ended by the power of Christian influence? How, then, can the Spirit of Christ, the Spirit of the gospel, be blamed? Will you attribute the darkness to the sun? Will you blame the filthiness of swine to the crystal-clear stream? Will you blame the fresh breeze from the sea for insect pests? To do so would be just as foolish.

Instead, we admit the darkness and the sin and the misery

---

5 Augeas was a king in Greek mythology who was known for having stables that had the most cattle in the country, but which had never been cleaned – until Heracles showed up and cleaned them.

of men. *Oh that my head were waters, and mine eyes a fountain of tears, that I might weep day and night!* (Jeremiah 9:1). But these are not the work of the Spirit of God. These come from the spirit from beneath. He who is from above would heal them. He is not limited. These are not because of Him. Where His gospel has been preached, and people have believed it and lived according to it, they have been enlightened, sanctified, and blessed. Life and love, light and liberty, and all other good things come from the Spirit of the Lord.

> Blessings abound where'er He reigns;
> The prisoner leaps to lose his chains,
> The weary find eternal rest,
> And all the sons of want are blest.[6]

---

6   This stanza is from Isaac Watts' hymn "Jesus Shall Reign Where'er the Sun," based on Psalm 72.

Chapter 4

Only Christ

If any of us would receive an assignment for Christian service, it must come from Christ Himself. If we would carry out that assignment, it must be in loyalty to Christ. If we hope to succeed in that assignment, we must do so while in perpetual, personal fellowship with Christ. We must begin to work with Him, continue working with Him, and never stop working until He Himself comes to discharge us from the service because there is no further need of it. Oh, that we did all our work in the name of the great Head of the church! Oh, that we did all Christ's work consciously in the presence and in the strength of Christ!

At this moment, Jesus possesses a royal authority – by might, it is true, but mainly by right. His power comes from His merits, from His glorious nature, and from the gift of the divine Spirit who rests upon Him without measure. The word that we translate "power" has a wider meaning than that. You find a good example of it in John 1:12: *As many as received him, to them gave he power to become the sons of God*, where the word "power" might be translated "privilege" or "right" or "liberty," and yet is also correctly translated as "power."

Jesus at this moment has all rights in heaven and in earth. He has all sovereignty and dominion, and of course, He has all the might that backs up His right; but it is not mere power in the sense of force. It is not the dynamite power in which earthly kings delight. It is another and a higher kind of force that Christ has; it is the divine energy of love. He possesses at this moment all authority in heaven and in earth.

All power, He says, *is given unto Me* (Matthew 28:18); that is to say, He has it now. You and I are not sent out to preach the gospel in order to get power for Christ; He has it now. We are not sent out, as we sometimes say, to win the world for Christ; in the strictest sense, it is His now. He is the King of Glory at this very moment. He is even now Lord over all, King of Kings and Lord of Lords. All authority is given unto Him. I will not try to explain the specific time when it was given, but I remind you that it has been given. That great act is accomplished. Our Lord Jesus holds in His hand the scepter that gives Him power over all flesh, that He may give eternal life to as many as the Father has given Him. He already has in His hand that scepter with which He will break the nations as with a rod of iron and dash them in pieces (Psalm 2:9). He does not have to go up to His throne, for He is already enthroned. He does not need to be crowned, for He is already crowned, as we have said, King of Kings and Lord of Lords.

I have met with some who have tried to read the Bible the wrong way upwards. They have said, "God has a purpose that is certain to be fulfilled; therefore, we will not budge an inch. All power is in the hands of Christ; therefore we will sit still." However, that is not Christ's way of reading the passage. His way is, "*All power is given unto Me,* therefore go and do something."

"But, Lord, what do You want from us when You have all power? We are such poor insignificant, useless creatures that we will be sure to mess up anything that we attempt."

"No," says the Master. "*All power is given unto Me*; therefore go."

Jesus tells us to go because He has all power. I know that with many of us there is a tendency to sit down and say, "All things are wrong, the world keeps getting worse and worse, and everything is getting bad." We sit and worry together in most delightful misery, trying to cheer each other downwards into greater depths of despair! Do we not often act like this? Sadly, it is so, and we feel happy to think that other people will blend in blessed harmony of misery with us in all our dejection. If we do try to do a little, we feel that there is not much good in our service and that very little can possibly come of it.

> The battle has begun, and every good soldier of Jesus Christ must be at the front for his Captain and his Lord.

This message of our Master seems to me to be like the sound of a trumpet. I have given you the strains of a wind chime, but now there rings out the clarion note of a trumpet. Here is the power to enable you to go. Therefore, go away from your garbage dumps, away from your ashes and your dust. Shake yourselves from your despair. The bugle calls, "Get ready to go! Charge!" The battle has begun, and every good soldier of Jesus Christ must be at the front for his Captain and his Lord. Because all power is given unto Christ, He passes on that power to His people and sends them forth to battle and to victory.

"Go, go," says Christ.

"But, Lord, if we go to men, they will ask for our passports and travel permits."

"Take them," Jesus says. "All authority and *all power is given unto Me in heaven and earth.* You are free of heaven, and you are free of earth. There is no place – whether it is in Ethiopia, in the deserts of the Middle East, or in the center of Rome – there is no place where you may not go. Here is your passport: 'All authority is given unto Me; therefore go.'"

"But, Lord, we need more than passports, we need a commission – an order from you."

"Here is your commission," says the Lord: "*All power is given unto Me*, and I delegate it to you. I have authority, and I give you authority; go, therefore, because I have the authority. Go and teach princes and kings and beggars – teach them all. I appoint you. I authorize you, as many of you as know Me and have My love shed abroad in your hearts, I commission you to go and 'Tell to sinners round what a dear Savior [you] have found,'⁷ and if they ask how you dare to do it, do not tell them that the bishop ordained you or that you are a licensed minister, but tell them that all power is given to your Master in heaven and in earth, and you have come in His name, and nobody may tell you otherwise."

"Moreover," says the Master, "I send you with My power already sent before you."

Pay attention to that, for I bring it again to your remembrance. Jesus does not say, "Go and win the power for Me on earth; go and get power for Me among the sons of men." No. He says, "I have already been given all authority and power, so therefore go. I do not send you to a country that is a foreign kingdom, but I send you to a country that is mine, for all souls are mine. If you go to the Jews or to the Gentiles, they are mine. If you go to India or China, you do not need to ask anyone's permission; you are in your own King's country. You are on a mission for your own King. You have your own King's power going before you."

I believe that when missionaries go to a country, they often gather ripe fruit rather than plant trees. As the Lord sent the

---

7   This line is from the hymn "Jesus, My All, to Heaven Is Gone," by John Cennick (1718-1755).

hornets to clear the way for the children of Israel, so He often sends notable political, social, and religious changes before the messengers of the cross to prepare the way for them. This is the message that clearly sounds to all the soldiers of King Jesus: "I have all authority in heaven and in earth; therefore, with confidence and without hesitation or doubt, *go ye therefore and teach all nations, baptizing them in the name of the Father and of the Son and of the Holy Spirit*" (Matthew 28:19).

Unless the Holy Spirit blesses the Word, we are the most miserable of all people, for we have attempted a task that is impossible and have entered upon an area where nothing but the supernatural will ever avail. If the Holy Spirit does not renew hearts, we cannot do it. If the Holy Spirit does not regenerate them, we cannot. If He does not send the truth home into their souls, we might as well speak into the ear of a corpse. All that we have to do is quite beyond our unaided power; we must have our Master with us, or we can do nothing. We deeply feel our need of this great truth. We do not merely say it, but we are driven every day by our own deep sense of need to rejoice that our Lord has declared, *All power is given unto me in heaven and in earth.*

Why are we ever downhearted? Why do we ever begin to question the ultimate success of the good cause? Why do we ever go home troubled and anxious because of the evils of the day? Courage, courage! The King has all power, it is impossible to defeat Him. The right wing of our army may be shattered for a moment, but the King in the center of the army still rides upon the white horse of victory, and He has but to will it – He only has to speak a single word – and the enemy will be driven away like chaff before the wind.

Christ says, "Go." Alright, then. Let us go at once, according to His Word, in the path that God's own hand marks out for us. Let us go and disciple all nations. Let us tell them that they need to learn about Jesus Christ and that they are to be obedient to His will.

Next, let us be loyal to Him in all things, and let us train up His disciples to be loyal to Him, *teaching them to observe all things whatsoever I have commanded you* (Matthew 28:20). As He has all authority, let us not bring in another authority. Let us stay within the Master's house and seek to know the Master's mind, learn the Master's will, study the Master's Book, and receive the Master's Spirit. Let these be dominant over all other powers. All the while, let us strive to remain in fellowship with Him.

Behold, I am with you always, He tells us (Matthew 28:20). Let us never go away from Him. Because all authority is given unto Him, let us stay close by His side; let us be the soldiers of His guard. Let us be the servants who unloose the straps of His sandals, who bring water for His feet, and who count ourselves highly honored to serve Him. *Behold, I am with you always,* He says, so let us always be with Him.

Chapter 5

Great Faith and Great Works

Where is your faith? (Luke 8:25)

T
hose nine disciples who remained at the foot of the mountain when the Savior took the other three to behold His transfiguration each had a true call from the Lord Jesus Christ. They were nine of His chosen apostles. He had chosen them according to His own good will and pleasure, and there was no doubt that they were really called to the apostleship. They were not only chosen, but they were also qualified, for on earlier occasions they had healed the sick, cast out devils, and had preached the Word of Christ with great power. Miraculous influences rested upon them, and they were able to do great wonders in the name of the Lord Jesus Christ. Not only were they qualified to do this, but they had actually performed many marvels of healing. When they went forth, clothed with divine power, they healed the sick and cast out devils everywhere; yet on this occasion they were completely baffled and beaten.

A poor father had brought to them his epileptic son, who was also possessed with an evil spirit. The disciples could neither cast out the evil spirit nor heal the epileptic boy. They came, as it were, to a great difficulty which quite perplexed them.

The scoffing scribes were there, ready to take advantage of the situation and to say in scorn and contempt, "You cannot cure this child, for the power you have received from your Master is limited. He can do some strange things, but even He cannot do all things. Perhaps He has lost His former power, and now, at last, a kind of devil has appeared that He cannot master. You are mistaken in following Him; you have placed your faith upon an impostor, and you had better give it up."

Oh, how ready the evil spirit always is to suggest dark thoughts if we cannot always be successful in our work of faith and labor of love! Why do you think that the Lord allows His servants to be defeated at all? Well, of course, the main reason in this case was because God gives the victory to faith, and if we will not believe, neither will we be established. If we fall, as those disciples probably had fallen, into an unspiritual frame of mind and a low state of grace, our orders will not be worth much, our former qualifications will be of little value, and all successes we have had in earlier days will not take away the effect of present failures. We will be like Samson, who went out and shook himself as he had done before, but the Spirit of God had departed from him and the Philistines soon overcame him – those very Philistines whom, if his Lord had still been with him, he would have smitten hip and thigh with great slaughter.

If we are to do the Lord's work successfully, we must have faith in Him. We must look beyond ourselves, beyond our mission, beyond our personal qualifications, and beyond our former successes. We must look for a current anointing by the Holy Spirit, and by faith we must depend upon the living God from day to day.

If I am successful, why is it that I succeed? Let me know the secret so I can put the crown on the right head. If I do not succeed, let me know the reason why so that I may at any rate try to remove any hindrance if it is one of my own making. If

I am a vessel that is not ready for the Master's use, let me know why I am not ready and why I am not prepared, that I may, as much as lies in me, prepare myself for the great Master's service. I know that if I am ready and prepared to be used, He will certainly use me. If He does not use me, it will most probably be because there is some unfitness in me. Try to know why you are hindered in your holy service for God, for it will be wise to know.

It may very well lead to you being humbled. It may make you go, with tears in your eyes, to the mercy seat. You may not yet know all that is in your own heart. There may be something that seems to you to be a very little thing, but it is grieving your God and weakening your spiritual power. It may seem to you to be a little matter, but in that little thing may lie the source of so much disobedience or damage that God will not tolerate it, and He will not bless you until you are completely rid of it.

> If He does not use me, it will most probably be because there is some unfitness in me.

It will be wise and right, therefore, even though it might be to your sorrow and regret, that you should find the answer to the question, *Why could not we cast him out?* (Matthew 17:19). I am sure that anything that makes us often come back to our Lord must be a blessing to us. It is very humiliating to have preached so long in vain, to have gone to that village so many times and yet see no conversions, to visit that boarding house so often and apparently to have made no impression upon the careless residents, or to have gone into that gloomy apartment and told the story of the cross – only to find that the hearer is just as dark and as brutal as ever.

It seems as if our hearts must break when we are really in earnest, yet we cannot achieve the blessed purpose that we feel certain must be dear to the Savior's own heart; but it may be that our lack of success has much divine instruction in it, and it may be the beginning and preparation for future success that will greatly honor the Lord Jesus Christ. This was part of the training of the twelve disciples. They were at college now, with Christ as their tutor. They were being prepared for those wonderful days when they would do even greater things than He had done, because He had gone back to His Father, had received still greater power, and had given it to them. *It is good for a man that he bear the yoke in his youth* (Lamentations 3:27).

Whatever the reason for your failure might be, it can be cured. In all probability, it is not a great matter, and it is certainly not an insurmountable difficulty to the Lord. By the grace of God, this hindrance can be taken away from you and no longer be allowed to rob you of your power. Search it out, then. Look with both your eyes and search with the brightest light that you can find, that you may find every reason that holds back the Spirit of God and diminishes your own usefulness.

"Why could we not cast the evils out of them?" Each Sunday school teacher can ask that question about his class, and each Christian worker about his sphere of labor. I ask it about some who have made a profession of Christianity but then have fallen into sin, and about others who have backslidden into coldness or lukewarmness, and about many who, after hearing years of preaching, remain just the same as ever. What devil is this that has got into them? Why cannot we cast him out?

The Lord Jesus told them that their failure was due to their lack of faith. He did not say, "Because of the devil and his poor character and the strength of his entrenchment within the poor sufferer's nature," but He said, *Because of your unbelief* (Matthew 17:20).

They could have said, and it would have been true, "This demon has been in him for a long time." The father said that the affliction came upon him when he was a child. You know that it is not easy to turn out a devil that has lived in any place, say, for twenty years. It is a difficult thing to get rid of sins and evils that have been around for a long time, but if we have faith, there will be no difficulty in overcoming even those sins that have held possession of the sinner for a long time.

Moreover, in this case, there was the strength of this demon as well as the length of his possession. He took this poor child and threw him into the fire or into the water and shook him back and forth at his cruel and wicked pleasure. He did this even while the disciples were watching. Yes, but if they had more faith, they would have understood that although Satan is strong, Christ is far stronger. The devil is mighty, but God is almighty. If the disciples had only believed, they might have overcome the demon by the power of Christ.

The lack of faith breaks the connection between us and Christ. We are like the landline telephone wire. It can carry the message as long as it can travel through the wire, but if you break the connection, it is useless. Faith is our connection with Christ. If the connection is broken, then what can we do? It is by faith that God works in us and through us, but if unbelief comes in, we are unfit for Him to work with us. Would you expect God to bless the person who will not believe in Him? Would you expect God to set His seal to the works of the unbelieving? That cannot be. The first condition of success in any work for God must be sincere faith in the God for whom we are working.

Looking now upon the condition of our times and upon the work assigned to each one of us, I feel that what we need is more faith. Never mind how firmly the mountains of iniquity are established; they must move if faith is strong. Never mind how deep the roots of the sycamine tree have gone;[8] it will be plucked up by its roots if faith is strong. *The Lord said, If ye had*

---

8   The sycamine tree is mentioned in the Bible only in Luke 17:6, and is thought
     to be a type of mulberry tree, probably the black mulberry.

faith as a grain of mustard seed, ye might say unto this sycamine tree, Be thou plucked up by the root, and be thou planted in the sea; and it should obey you (Luke 17:6). We do not half believe! You can plan and try and work on your own, but you will not succeed unless you simply trust your God as a child trusts his father. We have often failed because of our unbelief.

It may be that there are cases in which God will not give way to your faith until your faith works in prayer; and then, when prayer has worked to its utmost, you will get the blessing.

I think that I can understand some of God's reasons for doing this. First, He wants to make us see the greatness of His mercy, so He occupies our thoughts with the greatness of the distress that needs to be relieved. He wants us to see the impossibility of that distress being relieved except by His own power and Godhead. That experience does us good. It makes us feel that the mercy, when it does come, will be incredibly precious.

> It may be that there are cases in which God will not give way to your faith until your faith works in prayer.

The Lord intends also to stir us up to holiness, and that, likewise, does us good. To be all ablaze with holy desires is in itself a healthy exercise. Then the Lord means to create in us unity of action. One brother finds that he cannot get on alone, so he will call in another to help him in prayer. Much holy united supplication will be called forth by the very desperateness of the case that cannot be met by simple faith, or even by the prayer of one. Let us always seek the united prayers of many brothers and sisters.

Do you remember that man who was carried by four friends and was lowered down from the roof into Christ's presence (see Mark 2:1-12)? Oh, I wish that you met frequently together in your houses for united prayer! I would like to hear of little groups of Christian men and women who have pledged themselves to pray, four at a time, for somebody possessed by a devil of the kind that will not go out by ordinary means, and must be cast out by four of you. Get together and say to yourselves, "We will not rest until this person and that person has the devil cast out and has come to Christ, and is sitting, clothed, and in their right mind, at Jesus Christ's feet."

This kind. These certain kinds of devils are not to be driven out, except by special, persistent, continued, united prayer. They *can* be cast out if you only believe and pray. There is never a demon or an evil that will not have to go – if you have faith enough and prayer enough to drive it out.

By prayer and fasting. Our Lord Jesus Christ never made much of fasting. He very seldom spoke about it, and when the Pharisees exaggerated it, He generally put them off by telling them that the time had not come for His disciples to fast, because the Bridegroom was still with them, and while He was with them their days were to be days of joy. But still, Holy Scripture does speak of fasting. In certain cases it advises fasting, and there were godly men and women, such as Anna, the prophetess, who *served God with fastings and prayer night and day* (Luke 2:37).

I do not mean to spiritualize this away. I believe, literally, that some of you would be a great deal better off if you occasionally had a whole day of fasting and prayer. There is a lightness that comes over the frame, especially of bulky people like myself; we begin to feel quite light and graceful. I remember one day of fasting and prayer in which I realized to myself, spiritually, the meaning of a Roman Catholic picture, which I have sometimes seen, of a saint floating in the air. Well, that, of course, was impossible, and I do not suppose that, when the picture was painted, it was believed in its literal sense; but there is a lightness, an elevation of the spirit above the flesh, that will come over you after some hours of waiting upon God in fasting and prayer.

I can advise Christians sometimes to try it; it will be good for their health, and it certainly will not harm them. If we only ate about half of what is ordinarily eaten, we would probably all be in better health. If, occasionally, we would eat less food for a period of time, not because there is any virtue in that, but in order to get our brains more clear and to help our hearts to rest more fully upon the Savior, we would find that prayer and fasting have much power.

Allow me to say just one thing more. I believe that the demon of drunkenness will not go out of some people unless Christians who pray for them and talk with them will practice fasting in the matter of total abstinence. I do not mean that it is wrong for you to pray for them and try to help them, but there are some souls that you cannot win unless you say to them, "For your sakes we are going to give up what might be lawful to us, that we may save you from the taverns and all its temptations. Come, Jack. I intend to take the abstinence pledge. I was never drunk and probably never will be, but I will sign the pledge for your sake."

There are some demons and sins that will not leave until you act like that, and we should do anything that we can that might result in the saving of a soul. We ought to deny ourselves anything that we can deny ourselves, if it is necessary to bring one single person to the cross of Christ. Let us see to it that we are quite clear in this matter, for there are still many demons that will not go out without prayer and fasting.

Say, then, "I will not fast to please the devil or to please other people, but I will fast to displease the devil and to get him out of that person. I will fast from anything so that I may but bring him to the feet of Jesus so that he may be saved." We who love the Lord are, I trust, all agreed on that matter, that no cost on our part should be spared to win a soul from the dominion of Satan and to bring him into the glorious liberty of the children of God.

Chapter 6

Being Faithful with the Talents He Already Gave Us

He called him, and said unto him, How is it that I hear this of thee? give an account of thy stewardship. (Luke 16:2)

Give an account of your stewardship as to your talents. We all vary in natural gifts and skills. One person has the tongue of eloquence, another the pen of a ready writer, and a third the artistic eye that discerns beauty; but whichever of these we may have, they belong to God and ought to be used in His service.

Some only have such gifts as qualify them to earn their daily bread by manual labor. They do not have great mental power, yet they must give an account to God for what they have, and also for the physical strength with which God has blessed them. There is no person without a talent of some sort or other. There is no one without some form of power either given by nature or acquired by education. We are all equipped in some degree or other, and we must each give an account to God for that talent.

What an account some people must give who have been endowed with ten talents but have wasted them all! What must be the account rendered by a Napoleon? What must be the reckoning given by a Voltaire, with all the splendor of his intellect laid at the feet of Satan and desecrated to the damnation of mankind?[9] Yet while you think of these great ones of the earth, do not forget yourselves. What has been your special gift? You can speak well enough in the company of some people, but have you ever spoken for Christ? You can write well and you realize that you have a good gift in that area, but have you ever written a line that will bring your fellow men to the service of the Savior?

What! Having ten talents, are they all wrapped up and buried? Are they all used for self? Are none used for God, for holiness, for truth, and for righteousness? How sternly the command comes, *Give an account of thy stewardship*, yet I am afraid that none of us can give an account of our talents without fear and trembling.

Give an account of your substance. We vary greatly as to worldly circumstances. I suppose there are a few to whom God has entrusted great wealth, some to whom He has given considerable substance, and that to most He has given somewhat more than is absolutely necessary for actual needs; but whether it is much or little, we must give an account for it all. I do not know what some rich Christians will have to say concerning that which they give to the cause of God. They do not give God ten percent of what they have, but it is more like they give their table scraps, and these they only give for the sake of appearance because it would not look respectable if they were to give nothing at all.

The church's funds would never be as empty as they are if it

---

9   Voltaire, considered an atheist by many, was a French writer, historian, and philosopher known for his attacks against Christianity and his anti-God beliefs.

were not that some of the stewards in the church are not faithful to their trust. It is very sad to think of some of the prominent people in our own country who have incomes which, in a single month, would furnish a competent support for an entire family during their whole lives. I wonder what sort of reckoning theirs will be when they have to give an account of hundreds of thousands or even millions of dollars. With some of them, all they can say will be, "I lost so much on sports and entertainment, I spent so much on someone I was dating, I paid so much for diamonds, so much squandered in this form of waste, and so much in that." But for the poor and needy who are perishing in our streets, the multitudes who crave even necessary bread, some of them have done nothing at all.

There are wonderful exceptions, names that will live as long as philanthropy is prized among mankind; but the exceptions are so extremely few, that when the rich men of America and England and the rest of the world are indicted at the judgment seat of God, as they certainly will be, the account of their stewardship will be a truly terrible one.

Yet what are you, and what am I, to judge these things, if we cannot say that we have been faithful with what God has given to us? I ask if you have, and I pray that you will, make an evaluation in your mind now of your stewardship of the gold, silver, or copper with which God has entrusted you.

We must give an account of our influence. Everybody has some kind of influence. The mother who never leaves the nursery has a wonderful influence over her little children, although no neighbor feels the force of her influence and no one but her own little ones are affected by her faithfulness. Who knows but that she is perhaps caring for a Whitefield,[10] who will thunder

---

10   George Whitefield (1714-1770) was an English evangelist who was one of the early Methodist leaders. He preached in England and America, as well as in Scotland, Ireland, and a few other countries, and was one of the main preachers in America's first Great Awakening.

out the gospel through the length and breadth of the land; or perhaps, on the other hand, she might be taking care of an infidel, whose dreadful blasphemies will ruin multitudes? There is an influence that the mother has for which she must give an account to God.

And the father's influence – oh, fathers! You cannot dismiss your obligations to your children by sending them to school or even to a Sunday school. They are your children, and you must give an account of your stewardship concerning your own offspring. Not only the politician who thrills an audience with his oratory, but also he who speaks a word from the carpenter's bench – each has his influence, and each must use it and give an account of it.

It is not just the man who, by refusing to lend his millions, could prevent the horrors of war, but it is also the man who with a smile might help to laugh at sin, or with a word of rebuke might show that he abhorred it. There is not one of you without influence, and I ask you now how you have used it. Has it always been on the side of the Lord? *Give an account of thy stewardship*, for that influence will not always last.

We might consider other things that God has entrusted to us, but time would fail; so I remind you that the account that you will have to give, and that which I ask you to consider now, is not an account concerning other people. Wouldn't it be nice if we had to do that? With what enthusiasm some would undertake the task if they had to give a report of other people's characters! How easily each of us can play the detective upon our fellows! How ready we are to say of this man, "Oh, yes! He gives away a good deal of money, but it is only because he likes to show off." How ready we are to say of that woman, "Yes, she appears to be a Christian, but you do not know her private life," or of that minister of the gospel, "Yes, he is very zealous, but he has a comfortable life and has many advantages from his ministry."

We like to evaluate our fellow humans this way, and our evaluations are wonderfully accurate – at least we think so; but when other people evaluate us according to the same rule, we think their calculation seems terribly out of order, and we cannot believe it to be right. Ah! But at the great judgment we will not be asked to give an account for others, and I will not ask any of you now to think about the conduct of others.

So what if others are worse than you are; does that make you better or less guilty? What if others are not all they seem to be? Maybe you are not, either. At any rate, their hypocrisy will not make your deception to be true. Judge yourselves, so that you are not judged by others (see Matthew 7:1). Let each person clean his own wound and see to the affairs of his own soul, for each one must give an account of himself to God.

> Let each person clean his own wound and see to the affairs of his own soul, for each one must give an account of himself to God.

Remember, too, that you are not called upon to give an account of yourself to others. Alas! There are many who seem to live only to try to win the esteem of their fellows. There is somebody to whom we look up; if he or she only smiles at us, we think all is well. Maybe some are brokenhearted because that smile has vanished and they think they have been misjudged and unjustly condemned. It is a small matter to be judged according to man's judgment. *Who art thou that judgest another man's servant? to his own master he standeth or falleth* (Romans 14:4), and not to this interfering judge.

Remember, also, that the account to be given will be from everyone personally concerning himself; whatever another person's account of you may be, it will not affect you.

It was a saying of Pythagoras that each of his disciples should, every evening, give a record of the actions of the day. I think it is good to do so, for we cannot too often contemplate our actions and words. Sit down for a while, pilgrim; sit down for a while. Here is the milestone marked with the end of another year; sit down and think about it. Lay your hand upon your heart, and search and see what is there.

There is no one who so much dislikes to look at his bank account as he who is in debt or who is bankrupt. Those who keep no record, when they come before the court, are understood to be the most unprincipled people. Those who keep no mental notes of the past and bring up no recollections with regard to their sins, having tried to forget them all, may depend upon it that they are deceiving themselves. If you dare not search your hearts, I am afraid there is a reason for that fear, and that above all others you ought to be diligent in this search.

It may be that some may live for years, and yet are no longer stewards. A preacher may be set aside, his voice gone, his mental faculties weakened, and he is no longer a steward. One is thankful to have further opportunities of serving the Lord and trying to bring sinners to the Savior. Work for God while you can!

It is one of the bitterest regrets a man can know to lie on his bed, to be unable to speak, and to think to himself, "I wish I could preach that sermon over again. I did not drive that nail home with all the force I ought to have used. I have not been earnest enough in pleading with sinners. I have not wrestled to agony over the salvation of their souls." It may be possible that you and I may have twenty or thirty years before we are laid aside from active service; let us then work while we can, before the night comes when no one can work. *I must work the works of him that sent me, while it is day: the night cometh, when no man can work* (John 9:4). Let us seize the oar of the lifeboat and row out over the stormy sea, seeking to save the drowning ones from their shipwreck, for the time may come when our strong right arm will be paralyzed and we can do no more.

Also, wealthy Christians will have to give an account of their stewardship and may come to a point where they are no longer stewards. This happened to some people when the financial panic came; though they had much before the stock market crash, they had nothing left afterward, so they could no longer be stewards of the wealth that had been taken from them. It must be a cause of deep regret to people in that position if they cannot give a good account of their stewardship because they had not done much good with their wealth while they had it.

Do you to whom God has given great possessions consider how soon He may take them from you? Riches do not abide forever. Behold, our wealth can seem to have wings and fly away. I know of no better way of clipping those wings than by giving generously to the cause of God and using all that you can in His service. It would be a subject for continual regret to you if you came to poverty – not just that you had descended in the social scale, for you could bear that if it came by mere misfortune through the providence of God – but if you felt, "I did not do what I should have done when I had wealth," that would be the arrow that would pierce you to the heart. It may be so with some. In any case, I feel that there are some who are poor because God will not lend His money where He knows that it will be locked up and not put out to good interest in His cause. What little you have is all hidden away, so the Lord will not trust you with more. He sees you are not fit to be one of His stewards. There are some, on the other hand, whom God has entrusted with much because He sees that they use it wisely in promoting the interests of His kingdom.

But, after all, to every man, whether he is rich or whether he is in Christian ministry, there may be a close of his stewardship before he dies. There may come a point when God says to you, *Thou mayest be no longer steward* (Luke 16:2). The mother who has her little children swept away one after another – this is the message to her: "You may no longer be steward." The teacher has his class scattered, or he is himself unable to go to the school; the word to him also is, "You may no longer be steward." The man who went to work and could have spoken to his fellow laborer is transferred, perhaps to another country, or he is placed in a position where he cannot speak freely to others; now he can no longer be steward.

Use all opportunities while you have them, strike while the iron is hot, serve God today while you can! Let each golden moment have its pressing service given to God, lest it should be said to you, *Thou mayest be no longer steward.*

But we will soon no longer be stewards in another sense, too. The hour must come for us to die. We have constant reminders that those who have served God faithfully cannot abide with us forever. One or another whom we have loved and honored turns in his account and passes to rest. So it will be in turn with the pastor, the deacons, and the elders. Do not put away the thought of that day, my fellow workers, as though you were immortal. It may come to us suddenly. No grey hairs may cover our heads, but we may be called upon to turn in our account while we are yet in the full strength of manly vigor.

What do you think? Could you gather up your feet in the bed and look into eternity without feeling the cold sweat of fear stand upon your brow? Could you face the great judgment seat and say, *I know whom I have believed, and am persuaded that He is able to keep that which I have committed unto Him against that day* (2 Timothy 1:12)? Could you say, *I have fought a good fight, I have finished my course, I have kept the faith* (2 Timothy 4:7)? God will be praised if we are able to say that! What monuments of mercy will you and I be if we are able to say this at the close of our service, and to hear our Lord say, *Well done, good and faithful servant; . . . enter thou into the joy of thy Lord* (Matthew 25:23).

Chapter 7

The Joy of the Lord's Harvest

Thou hast multiplied the nation, Thou hast increased their joy. (Isaiah 9:3, RV)

W e feel that we ought to be glad when others join the church, because we look back with great pleasure upon our own joining it. I remember the trouble it cost me to join the church. I think I went to see the pastor some four or five days in a row. He was always too busy to see me, until at last I told him it did not matter, for I would go to the church meeting and recommend myself as a member. Then, all of a sudden, he found time to see me, and so I managed to get into the church and confess my faith in Christ. That was one of the best day's work I ever did, when I openly declared my faith in Christ and united myself with His people! I think many could say the same; they remember when they united with the people of God and publicly declared their faith in Jesus Christ.

Conversion must be the Lord's work. The only multiplication of the church of God that is to be desired is that which God sends: *Thou hast multiplied the nation.* If we add to our churches by becoming worldly or by taking in people who have never been born again, or if we add to our churches by accommodating the life of the Christian to the life of the people of the world, our increase is worth nothing at all. It is a loss rather than a gain. If we add to our churches by excitement and by making appeals to the emotions rather than by explaining truth to the understanding, or if we add to our churches in any other way than by the power of the Spirit of God making people new creations in Jesus Christ, the increase is of no worth whatever.

A man picked himself up from the gutter and rolled up against Mr. Rowland Hill[11] one night as he went home. He said, "Mr. Hill, I am pleased to see you, sir. I am one of your converts."

Rowland said, "I thought it was very likely you were. You are not one of God's converts, or else you would not be drunk."

There is a great lesson in that answer. My converts are no good. Rowland Hill's converts could get drunk; but the converts of the Spirit of God, those who are really renewed in the spirit of their mind by a supernatural operation, these are a real increase to the church of God. *Thou hast multiplied the nation.* Pray hard that the Lord may continue to send us converts. He never sends the wrong people. However poor they may be, however illiterate – if they are converted, as they will be if the Lord sends them, they are the very people that we want. May God send us thousands more!

The people that walked in darkness have seen a great light: they that dwell in the land of the shadow of death, upon them hath the light shined (Isaiah 9:2). When God brings people to the church, they are the people who have undergone a very remarkable change. They have come out of unmistakable horrible darkness into marvelous and delightful light. God sends no other people than these. If you have not been changed by God, if you are not a new creation in Christ Jesus (2 Corinthians

11   Rowland Hill (1744-1833) was an English evangelical pastor.

5:17), if you cannot say, *One thing I know, that, whereas I was blind, now I see* (John 9:25), the church cannot receive you as you are, and God has not sent you.

Who can turn us from darkness unto light except God? Who can work this great miracle within the heart? Darkness of heart is very hard to move. Who but God can make the eternal light burst through the natural darkness and turn us from the power of Satan unto God?

Conversion must have a distinct relation to Christ. *For unto us a child is born, unto us a son is given: and the government shall be upon his shoulder: and his name shall be called Wonderful, Counsellor, the mighty God, the everlasting Father, the Prince of Peace* (Isaiah 9:6). We want converts who know this Christ, men and women to whom He is *Wonderful*, to whom He has become the *Counsellor*. We want no additions to the church of those who cannot call Him *the mighty God, the everlasting Father*. We want men and women to whom Christ has become *the Prince of Peace*. If these are added to us, the church grows exceedingly. If others are added, they do but increase our burden and become our weakness; in many cases they become our disgrace.

The joy of any growing church will be such as God gives. That is the kind of people we desire to have. If anyone wants to see the church grow so that we may outdo other churches, that is not the joy that God gives. If we like to see converts because we are glad that our opinions should be spread, God does not give that joy. If we desire converts so that we may steal them from other people, God does not give that joy, if it even is a joy. I do not think God loves sheep-stealers, and there are plenty of these around. We do not desire to increase our numbers by taking Christian people away from other Christian communities. No – the joy that God gives is clear, unselfish delight in Christ being glorified, in souls being saved, in truth being spread, and in error being corrected.

The farmer expects a harvest. He says, "It is so many weeks to harvest." He sows his seed with a view to harvest. He clears out the weeds with a view to harvest. He has a barn, and he has a threshing machine, all with a view to harvest. Well, now, every church should be looking out for a spiritual harvest. One pastor said to me once, "I have preached for several years, and I believe God has blessed the Word; but nobody ever comes forward to tell me so."

I said to him, "Next Lord's Day, say to the people, 'I will be in the vestry when the sermon is finished to greet friends who have been converted.'"

To his surprise, ten or twelve came in. He was quite surprised and, of course, delighted. He had not looked for a harvest, so of course he did not get it. My first student went out to preach on Tower Hill, Sunday after Sunday. He came to me, and said, "I have been out preaching now for several months on Tower Hill, and I have not seen one conversion."

I said to him rather sharply, "Do you expect that God is going to bless you every time you choose to open your mouth?"

He answered, "Oh! no, sir; I do not expect Him to do that."

"Then," I replied, "that is why you do not get a blessing."

We ought to expect a blessing. God has said that His Word will not return unto Him void (Isaiah 55:11), and it will not. We ought to look for a harvest. He who preaches the gospel with his whole heart ought to be surprised if he does not hear of conversions. He ought to begin to say in his heart, "I am determined to know the reason why," and never stop until he has found out. The joy of harvest is what we have a right to expect.

He is bound to rejoice in a harvest who has sorrowed in plowing, in sowing seed, in watching his crop when it was in the ear, and when frost, blight, and mildew threatened to destroy it. Many of us here can rejoice in the joy of harvest, because in those converted to Christ, we see the fruit of our soul's travail.

I find that I am very generally the spiritual grandfather of those who come, rather than their father in the faith; for I find that many of you, whom God gave me in years past, are diligent in seeking the souls of others. In the case of many who join the church, their conversion is due to this sister or to this brother, rather than distinctly to my ministry. I am very glad to have it so. I have recently spoken to two such friends, both of whom said to me, "I am your spiritual grandchild." One of these men was from America. I asked, "How is that?" The answer was, "Mr. So-and-so, whom you brought to Christ, came out to America, and he brought me to Christ."

It is a joy that has solid ground to go upon. I do not know of a more joyful occasion than when young men and women, and for that matter, old men and women, too, are brought to confess Christ and to unite with His people. It is a very joyful thing to attend a wedding, but it is always a matter of speculation as to how it will turn out; however, when you come to see a soul surrender to Christ, there is no speculation about that. You have a blessed certainty.

I think the angels sing more sweetly than ever as they hear a man, woman, or child say, "I trust in Jesus; I confess His name." When we know and believe that true faith in Christ means present salvation, there is a great joy about that. I heard of some preachers who say that there is no such thing as a present salvation. Though they constantly preach, they tell the people every now and then that they might be able to be saved when they come to die, but there is no such thing as being saved now. I would like to present those brethren with a little "Catechism for the Young and Ignorant," which Mr. Cruden liked to give away; for if they are not young, they certainly must be ignorant of the first principles of the faith. You are saved if you have believed in Christ Jesus. You are saved even now. If you were not, I do not see any reason why we should rejoice over you with the joy of harvest.

This is a joy in which many may join, for in the harvest, anybody who likes may rejoice. There is the owner of the field; he rejoices. How greatly Christ rejoices! There are the laborers; they shout as they bring home the loads of wheat, for they know the labor that has gone into that field of wheat.

Let us who are working for Jesus have the joy of harvest. The onlookers, too, as they go by and see the harvest gathered in, will stop and even give a shout over the hedge. If you are not yourself saved, you might be glad that other people are. Even if you are not yourself going to heaven, rejoice that others are choosing the blessed road. I invite even you to come and share the joy of harvest with us. The gleaner over there in the field says, "I have stooped many times. I have almost broken my back over the work, and I have only picked up this little handful." I know you, sister, and I am pleased that you would bring even one to Christ. I know you, brother, and I rejoice with you that you would bring even one child to the Savior. Though you are but a gleaner, join wholeheartedly with us in the joy of harvest.

What do we say of those who never sow? Well, they will never reap; they will never have the joy of harvest. Am I addressing any professing Christians who never sow, never speak a word for Christ, never visit a house and try to introduce the Savior's name, never seek to bring children to the Savior, and take no part in teaching Sunday school or in other service for Christ?

Do I address some lazy man here, spiritually alive only for himself? Oh, poor soul, I would not like to be you, because I doubt whether you can be spiritually alive at all! Certainly he who lives for himself is dead while he lives, and you will never know the joy of bringing souls to Christ. When you get to heaven, if you ever do get there, you will never be able to say,

"Here am I, Father, and the children whom You have given to me." You will have to abide eternally alone, having brought no fruit to God in the form of converts from sin. Shake yourselves up, brothers and sisters, from sinful sloth!

"Oh!" someone says, "I am not my brother's keeper." No, I will tell you your name; it is Cain. You are your brother's murderer, for every professing Christian who is not his brother's keeper is his brother's killer, and you can be sure that it is so. You can kill by neglect quite as surely as you can kill by the bow or by the dagger.

What do we say to those who have never reaped? Well, that depends. Perhaps you have only just begun to sow. Do not expect to reap before God's time. *In due season we shall reap, if we faint not* (Galatians 6:9). There is a set season for reaping; but if you have been sowing seeds for a very long time and you have never reaped, may I ask the question, Where do you buy your seeds? If I were to sow my garden year after year and nothing ever came up, I would change where I buy my seeds. Perhaps you have bad seed and have not sown the gospel pure and undiluted. You have not brought it out in all its fullness. Go to the Word of God and get *seed for the sower* of a kind that will feed your own soul, for it is *bread for the eater.*

For as the rain cometh down, and the snow from heaven, and returneth not thither, but watereth the earth, and maketh it bring forth and bud, that it may give seed to the sower, and bread to the eater: So shall my word be that goeth forth out of my mouth (Isaiah 55:10-11). When you sow that kind of seed, it will come up.

> Shake yourselves up, brothers and sisters, from sinful sloth!

Chapter 8

The Body Works Together

For the body is not one member, but many.
(1 Corinthians 12:14)

To have a noble purpose and to pursue that purpose with all your might prevents your being like "dumb driven cattle," lifts you out of the mist and fog of the valley, and sets your feet upon the hilltop, where you can commune with God. I would suggest to our younger friends that they should begin their Christian life with a high purpose and that they would never forget that purpose. If trouble should come, they should say, "Let it come; my face is set like a flint to do this work to which my Lord has called me, and I will pursue it with all my might." It may seem as if there is no spiritual help in such advice as this, but believe me, there is. If God will give you grace to go on with your life's work, He will thereby give you grace to overcome your life's trouble.

David's work is added on to by the work of another. That should be a great joy to some of you who do not see much coming of what you are doing. Your work is going to be added on to by somebody else's work.

This is the order of God's providence in His church. It does not often happen that He gives an entire piece of work to one man; rather, He seems to say to him, "You go and do so much, then I will send somebody else to do the rest." How this ought to cheer some of you up – the thought that your work may not be a failure (even though in itself it may seem to be so), because it will be added to by the work of somebody else who is coming after you; so it will be very far from a failure!

You have sometimes seen a person agree to put in the foundation of a house and to build it up to a certain height. He will do that, but he will not be the builder of that house. That will be the work of the next contractor, who builds the walls, puts on the roof, and so forth. Yes, but he who did the foundation work did a great deal, and he is as much the builder of the house as the person who builds the walls.

We do not live for honor, but we live to serve God.

I daresay that Solomon often thought gratefully of his father David and what he had done; and you and I, if God blesses us, ought always to think with thanksgiving of the Davids who went before us. If you have success in your Sunday school class, my sister, remember that there was an excellent Christian woman who had the class before you. You come, young man, into the Sunday school, and you think that you must be somebody very great because you have had several conversions in your class. How about the brother who had to give up the class because of poor health? You took his place. Who knows which of you will have the honor at the last great day?

Who cares who gets the credit? We do not live for honor, but we live to serve God. If I can serve God best by digging out the cellar, and you can serve God best by putting in that ornamental window, my brother, you go on with your window, and I will go on with my cellar, for what does it matter what we do as long as the house is built and God is glorified thereby? It is the way of God in providence to set one person to do part of a work that adds on to that of another person.

This is a terrible blow at self. Self says, "I like to begin something of my own, and I like to carry it out; I do not want any interference from other people." The other day, a friend proposed to give you a little help in your service. You looked at him as if he had been a thief. You do not want any help; you are quite up to the challenge. You are like a wagon and four horses, and a dog under the wagon as well! There is everything about you that is wanted. You do not need any help from anybody. You can do all things almost without the help of God!

I am very sorry for you if that is your opinion. If you get into God's service, He may say to you, "You will never begin anything, but you will always come in as the second man." Maybe God will say to you, "You will never finish anything; you will always be getting ready for somebody else." It is good to have an ambition not to build upon another man's foundation, but do not carry that idea too far. If there is a good foundation laid by another man, and you can finish the structure, be thankful that he has done his part – and rejoice that you are permitted to carry on his work. It is God's way of striking a blow at our personal pride by allowing one person's work to be joined to another's.

I believe that it is good for the work to have a change of workers. I am glad that David did not live any longer, for he could not build the temple. David had to die. He had a good time of service. He had gathered all the materials for the temple. Along comes Solomon, with young blood and youthful vigor, and carries on the work.

Sometimes the best thing that some of us old folk can do is to go home, go to heaven, and let some younger person come and do our work. I know there is much sorrow about the death of Dr. So-and-so and Mrs. So-and-so, but why? Do you not think after all, that God can find just as good servants as those He has found already? He made those good men, and He is not short of power; He can make others just as good as they have been.

I was present at a funeral where I heard a prayer that rather shocked me. Some brother had said that God could raise up another minister equal to the one who was in the coffin; but prayer was offered up by another man who said that this preacher had been eyes to his blindness, feet to his lameness, and I do not know what else beside. Then he said, "Your poor unworthy servant does not think that You ever can or will raise up another man like him." It seems as if he did not have an omnipotent God, but you and I have, and with an omnipotent God, it is for the good of the work that David should go to his rest and that Solomon should come in and carry on the work.

Certainly this creates unity in the church of God. If we all had a work of our own and were closed up by ourselves to do it, we would not know one another; but now I cannot do my work without your help, my dear friends, and in some respects, you cannot do your work without my help. We are members one of another, and one helps the other.

We need recruits. We are always looking for them. May God lead some who have been on the side of sin and self to come out and say, "Set my name down among God's people. By the grace of God, I am going to be on Christ's side and will help to build His temple." Come along, my brother. Come along, my sister. We are glad of your help. The work is not all done yet. You are not too late to fight the Lord's battles nor to win the victors' crown. The Lord has a large army of the soldiers of the cross, and *thou mayest add thereto* (1 Chronicles 22:14). May God save you! May Christ bless you! May the Holy Spirit inspire you!

Chapter 9

Merely a Servant

Behold, in my trouble I have prepared for the house
of the Lord an hundred thousand talents of gold,
and a thousand thousand talents of silver; and of
brass and iron without weight; for it is in abun-
dance: timber also and stone have I prepared; and
thou mayest add thereto. (1 Chronicles 22:14)[12]

The building of the temple is an admirable type of the building of the church of God. If you are workers for the Lord, if your hearts are right with God, I think that I will be able to say some things that will encourage you to work on, even if you do not now see any immediate results from your work.

There were many who helped to build the temple. David organized the gathering of the materials. Solomon, by whose name the temple would afterward be called, put it together, with the princes helping him in the great work, along with strangers, foreigners, and aliens who lived throughout Israel and Judah. These all had a part; even the Tyrians and Zidonians had a part in the work.

---

12   A talent in the times of biblical Israel is thought to have weighed about seventy-
    five pounds.

There are many servants of God whose names are little known, who nevertheless are doing a work that is essential to the building up of the kingdom of God. I have known many such people who have never lived to realize any great success. Their names have never been written upon any great temples that have been built, but nevertheless, they have admirably done their part, even as David did.

David gathered the materials. Many people gather people together, yet do not see their success. One man might be the founder of a Christian congregation, but he does not live to see many conversions. He gets together the raw material upon which another will work. He plows and he sows, but it takes another man to come and water the seed, and perhaps another to gather in the harvest. Still, the sower did his work and deserves to be remembered for what he did. David did his part of the work in getting together the materials for the temple.

David also had some of the materials for the temple made. He had the stones cut from the quarry and had many of them shaped to take their places, in time, in silence in the temple, when it would be built without sound of hammer or ax. Even so, there are teachers and preachers who help to form the characters of their scholars and hearers by working away upon their minds and hearts. They will never build up a great church, but still they are knocking the rough edges off the stones. They are preparing and forming them, and in time the builder will come and make good use of them.

David prepared the way for Solomon's temple. It was by his fighting that the time of peace came in which the temple could be erected. Though he is called a man of blood, it was needful that the enemies of Israel were overthrown. There could be no peace until her adversaries had been crushed, and David did that. You do not hear much about the men who prepare the way for others. Somebody else comes along and apparently does all the work, and his name is widely known and honored; but God remembers the messengers, the pioneers, the men who prepare the way, the men who, by casting out devils, confronting and defeating shameful errors, and promoting needful reforms, prepare the way for the triumphal progress of the gospel.

David found the site for the temple. He discovered it, he purchased it, and he handed it over to Solomon. We do not always remember the men who prepare the sites for the Lord's temples. Luther is rightly remembered, but there were Reformers before Luther. There were hundreds of men and women who were burned for Christ, perished in prison, or were put to cruel deaths for the gospel. Luther arrived when the occasion had been prepared for him and when a site had been cleared

It may be your duty to clear the site and prepare the way for others.

for him upon which to build the temple of God, but God also remembers all those pre-Reformation heroes. It may be your duty to clear the site and prepare the way for others. You might die before you see even a cornerstone of your own work laid, but it will be yours when it is finished, and God will remember what you have done.

It was David who received the plans from God. The Lord wrote upon his heart what He wanted done. He told him, even down to the weight of the candlesticks and lamps, everything that was to be arranged. Solomon, wise as he was, did not plan the temple. He had to borrow the designs from his father, who had received them directly from God. Many people can see far ahead. They get the plan of the gospel into their hearts, see a way in which great things can be done, and yet they are not permitted to put their own hands to the work. Another person will come along and carry out the plan that the first one received, but we must not forget the first man who went into the secret place of the Most High and learned in the place of thunder what God wanted His people to do.

David did one more thing: before he died, he gave a solemn exhortation to others. He instructed Solomon, the princes, and all the people to carry out the work of building the temple. I respect the man who, in his old age, when there is importance in every syllable that he utters, concludes his life by urging others to carry on the work of Christ. It is something special, when you are near the end of your life, to gather young men around you who have years of usefulness before them, and to lay upon their consciences and their hearts the duty of preaching Christ crucified and winning the souls of the lost for the Lord.

Oh, that each one would do his own part, even as David did his!

You see that David had done his part toward building the temple. Have you done your part? You are a child of God. God has loved you and chosen you. You have been redeemed with precious blood. You know better than to think of working in order to save yourself. You are saved, but have you diligently done all that you can do for your Lord and Master?

There is much else that you can do for Jesus Christ in your family, in your business, and in the neighborhood where you live. Could you go to bed tonight and close your eyes for the last time, feeling, "I have finished the work that God gave me to do. I have done all that I could in winning souls"?

I am afraid that some have a talent wrapped in a napkin, hidden away in the earth. Dig it up before it gets covered with rust and bears witness against you. Take it up and put it out to heavenly interest so that your Lord may have what He is entitled to receive. Christian men and women, there must be a lot of unused energy in the church of God! We have a great dynamo that is never used. Oh, that each one would do his own part, even as David did his!

We will soon be gone; our day does not last very long. *The night cometh, when no man can work* (John 9:4). Will it be said of you or of me that we wasted our daylight? Will it be said of us that when the evening shadows came, we were uneasy and unhappy, and though saved by divine grace, we died with sad expressions of regret for wasted opportunities?

Not very long ago, I sat by the bedside of one who was very wealthy. I prayed with him. I had hoped to have found him rejoicing in the Lord, for I knew that he was a child of God; but he was a child of God with a little deformity of the fingers – he could never open his hand as he ought to have done. As I sat by his side, he said, "Pray to God with all your might that I may live three more months, that I may have an opportunity of using my wealth in the cause of Christ." He did not live much more than three hours after he said that.

Oh, that he had woken up a little sooner to do for the Master's kingdom and cause what he ought to have done! Then he would not have had that regret to trouble him in his last hours. He knew the value of the precious blood, and he was resting in it. I had great joy in knowing that all his hope and all his trust were in his Lord, and he was saved, but it was with a great deal of regret and trembling. I want to spare any of you who have wealth such trouble on your dying bed.

If there is a young man who has the ability to preach the gospel or to be doing something for Christ, and he is doing nothing, I am sure that it will cause pain to him one of these days. When his conscience is thoroughly awake and his heart is getting nearer to God than it has been, he will bitterly regret that he did not take advantage of every opportunity to talk about Christ and to seek to bring souls to Him.

David had done his part in trouble. *Now, behold, in my trouble I have prepared for the house of the Lord an hundred thousand talents of gold.* In the margin of your Bibles, you might find the words, "in my poverty." It is strange that David would talk about poverty when his gifts amounted to many millions of dollars.

David thought little of what he had prepared. He calls it poverty, I think, because it is the way of the saints to consider anything that they do for God to be very little. The most generous men in the world think the least of what they give to God's cause. David, with his millions that he gives, says, *In my poverty I have prepared for the house of the Lord.* As he looked at the gold and silver, he said to himself, "What is all this to God?" When he considered the brass and the iron, that it could not be counted because it was so much and so costly, he thought it was all nothing to Jehovah, who fills heaven and earth and whose grandeur and glory are altogether unspeakable.

If you have done the most that you can for God, you will sit down and mourn that you cannot do ten times as much. You who do little for the Lord will be like a hen with one chick; you will think a great deal of it. But if you have a great number of works and you are doing much for Christ, you will wish that you could do a hundred times as much. Some Christians want to have all sunshiny weather, and the birds must sing all day and all night to please them. If they receive a rebuke, or if somebody seems a little cold to them, they will do no more. I have seen many people who called themselves Christians who were like silly children at play, who say, when something offends them, "I won't play anymore." They run away at the first rough word that they hear. But David, in the day of his trouble, when his heart was ready to break, still went on with his great work of providing for the house of God.

David prepared for the house of the Lord in his trouble, and I have no doubt that it was a comfort to his sorrow. To have something to do for Jesus and to go right on with it is one of the best ways to get over a bereavement – or any type of loss or sorrow. If you can pursue some great purpose, you will not feel that you are living for nothing. You will not sit down in despair, for whatever your trouble may be, you will still have this to live for: "I want to help build the kingdom of God, and I will do my part in it no matter what happens to me. Come poverty or wealth, sickness or health, life or death – as long as there is breath in my body, I will go on with the work that God has given me to do."

In many Christian works, you will have to do without me one of these days, but that will not matter. There will be somebody who will carry on the work of the Lord, and as long as the work goes on, what does it matter who does it? God buries the workman, but the devil himself cannot bury the work. The work is everlasting, even though the workmen die. We pass away as star after star grows dim, but the eternal light is never fading. God will have the victory. His Son will come in His glory. His Spirit will be poured out among the people, and though it might not be this man or that man or the other man, God will find the man who will carry on His cause until the end of the world and who will give to Him the glory.

Chapter 10

With God Nothing is Impossible

Is not the Lord your God with you? and hath he not given you rest on every side? for he hath given the inhabitants of the land into mine hand; and the land is subdued before the Lord, and before his people. (1 Chronicles 22:18)

Let every man and every woman among us judge of our lives, not merely from that little narrow piece of it which we ourselves live, for that is but a vapor, but let us judge it by its connection with other lives that may come after our own. If we cannot do all we wish, let us do all we can, in the hope that someone who will come after us may complete the project that is so dear to our heart.

That is a wonderful prayer that Moses wrote: *Let thy work appear unto thy servants, and thy glory unto their children* (Psalm 90:16). We will be quite satisfied to do the work without seeing much of the glory if we can know that in another generation the work that we will have done will produce glory to God that will be seen among the children of men. It is enough for us to do today's work this day; let somebody else do tomorrow's work if we are not around to do it. Today, do that which comes to your hand, and do not spend your time dreaming of the future. Put down that telescope. Why are you trying to gaze into the next hundred years? The important matter is not what you see with your eye, but what you do with your hand. Do it, and do it at once, with all your might, believing that God will find somebody else to go on with the next part of the work when you have finished your part.

There is also another delightful thought here, and that is the continuity of the divine blessing. God was with David in the gathering together of the great stores of treasure for the building of the temple; then God was also with Solomon. Oh, what a mercy it is that God did not give all His grace to other people before we came into the world! The God of grace did not empty the whole horn of grace upon the head of Whitefield or Wesley. He did not pour out all the blessings of His Spirit upon George Muller and John Newton so as to leave nothing for us. No – and to the end of time, He will be the same God as He was yesterday and as He is today. There is no break in the Lord's blessing. He has not ceased to be gracious. *The Lord's hand is not shortened, that it cannot save; neither his ear heavy, that it cannot hear* (Isaiah 59:1).

God buries His workmen, but His work goes on. He, the Great Worker, does not grow weary of it, nor will He ever fail or be discouraged. All His everlasting purposes will be accomplished. *He shall see of the travail of his soul, and shall be satisfied* (Isaiah 53:11). Wherefore, let us be of good heart if we have been inclined to look upon the future with fear. The Lord Jesus still lives, and He will take care that His church will live and work on until He Himself *shall descend from heaven with a shout, with the voice of the archangel, and with the trump of God* (1 Thessalonians 4:16).

We are engaged in building a temple in a spiritual sense. God has sent His servants into the world to gather together for His beautiful house stones hewn out of the quarry of humanity, to be shaped, polished, and prepared for building into the temple of His grace. The church is the living temple of God, *exceeding magnifical* (1 Chronicles 22:5). It is a wondrous idea that men's hearts and souls can be blended together and built up into a spiritual temple in which God will dwell. This temple is to be built from stones taken from the quarry of humanity, and God being with us, you and I are to go forth and to hew out and shape and prepare the stones for the building of this house of the Lord that will endure forever.

Is not the Lord your God with you? I will go any distance with the brother who likes to preach upon the inability of man and our utter and entire weakness apart

> Remember that when you are weak, then you are strong, if you will fall back upon the omnipotence of God.

from the Creator. You cannot, I think, exaggerate there; but do not always keep dwelling upon your own weakness. Remember that when you are weak, then you are strong, if you will fall back upon the omnipotence of God.

Is not the Lord your God with you? Has He sent us into the world with the gospel, and will He not be with us? Has He sent us to be the means of seeking souls, and has He made our hearts to ache because of the sins that people have committed against Him, and will He not be with us? Do not let us talk as if we had to live and labor without our God. We have been brought to know Him. We have been made members of the body of Christ, for the Holy Spirit dwells in us, if we are what we profess to be – the church of the living God. Will He not occupy the house that He has built? *Is not the Lord your God with you?* Then what can be too difficult for you?

It is the good pleasure of God to be with His people. He is our Father, and don't fathers love to be with their children? The loving father says, when he has little ones at home, "I will get back from my business early so that I can spend my evening with my family." We feel ourselves happiest when, laying aside external cares, we leave the world behind and rest with our loved ones at home.

God is at home with His people, and as our Father, He delights in His children. Remember how divine Wisdom said, *My delights were with the sons of men* (Proverbs 8:31). It is a wonderful thing to be able to say, but God takes a great deal more pleasure in us than we do in Him; yet there seems to be nothing in us that can give Him pleasure, while in Him there is everything that can provide us with delight. The Lord so loves His people that He is never long away from them.

A brother going out to Australia came to say goodbye to me. He gave me a little sketch of his life during his previous twenty-three years. Then he said, "Yes, sir, you drove me out to work for Christ; you would not let me be idle. You said, 'The worst kind of lazy people are lazy Christians,' and you also said that to come twice on a Sunday and hear you preach, and to be doing nothing for the Master, is not at all the right thing." Then the man added, "I do not often get to hear you now. I have been secretary of a Sunday school for some time, and I often go out preaching, so I cannot come to the Tabernacle." I delight in so many members not coming to hear us preach because they are doing the Master's work elsewhere!

I know that in many churches the main thing is to sit down in the back row and be fed. Well, of course every creature needs to be fed, from the pig upwards. You must excuse my mentioning that unclean animal, for he is the creature whose main business it is to be fed, and he is not a nice creature at all. I do not at all admire Christian people whose one business is to be fed. I have even heard them grumble about a sermon that was meant for the conversion of sinners, because they thought there was no food for them in it! They are great receptacles of food, but dear Christian people, not one of you should live merely to be fed – not even on heavenly food. If God is with you, as you say He is, then get to His work.

"What should I do?" someone asks. That is no business of mine. You have to find work for yourself. He who works for God does not need to go to this person or that person and ask, "What should I do?" Do the first thing that comes to hand, but get to work for your Master! Many Christians live in country villages where there is no preaching of the gospel; then preach it yourself. "Oh, but I could not!" Well then, get somebody who can. "But we have no chapel," someone says. What do you want with a chapel these bright days? Preach on the village green, where the old trees that were cut down a year or two ago are still lying there and will serve for seats.

"I could not preach," someone says. "I would break down." That would be an excellent thing to do; break-down sermons are often the best for breaking down other people as well as the preacher. Some of the greatest enterprises in the world have sprung from very little causes. The forest of the mightiest oaks in the world was once only a handful of acorns. Oh, that we might all do what we can for Him who laid down His life for us and who continues to abide in us, to be our joy and our strength!

David encouraged people to set their hearts upon what they had to do: *Now set your heart and your soul to seek the Lord your God* (1 Chronicles 22:19). Oh, how much there is of our religion that is a kind of celestial going to sleep! The preacher preaches as if he had not really woken up yet, and the people hear in the same way. Are there not, even in our churches, many who, if a coin or two were to jingle, would be sufficiently wide awake to look for it, but when the gospel is being preached, they are not thoroughly awake? As to speaking to strangers and saying a word for the Master, that has not yet occurred to them.

"I do not know what I can do," someone says. Brother, if the

Bible verse is true, I do not know what you cannot do. *Is not the Lord your God with you?* "Well, I could not—"

Could not? Could not? Do you put God and "could not" together? I think it would be infinitely better to put God and "can" or God and "will" together. If God is with us, what can be impossible? What can be even difficult for us? When God is with His people, *he that is feeble among them at that day shall be as David; and the house of David shall be as God, as the angel of the Lord before them* (Zechariah 12:8).

Chapter 11

We Must Bear Fruit

The fig tree putteth forth her green figs, and the
vines with the tender grape give a good smell.
(Song of Solomon 2:13)

The vine is of all trees the most useless unless it bears fruit. You can make hardly anything of it. You would hardly be able to cut enough wood out of a vine to hang a pot upon it. You cannot turn it into furniture, and you could barely use it in the least degree for building purposes. It must either bear fruit or be consumed in the fire. The branches of the vine that bear no fruit are necessarily cut off, and they are used, as I have seen them used in the south of France many times, in little twisted bundles for kindling a fire. They burn very rapidly, so there is soon an end of them, and then they are gone.

The vine is constantly used in the Bible as a picture of the nominal church of Christ; so, like the vine, we must either bring forth fruit or we will be accounted as good for nothing. We must serve God. We must bring forth, from our very soul, love to God and service to Him as the fruit of our renewed nature, or else we are useless, worthless, and will only abide our time before being cut down to be burned. Our end will be destruction if our life is not fruitful.

This gives a very solemn importance to our lives, and it should make each of us seriously ask, "Am I bringing forth fruit unto God? Have I brought *forth fruits meet for repentance?*" (Matthew 3:8). For if not, you must soon feel the sharp edge of the Vinedresser's knife and will be taken away from any sort of union that you now have with the church, which is Christ's vine, and will be flung over the wall as a useless thing whose end is to be burned.

We must bear fruit or we will certainly perish. We cannot have fruit unless we have Christ. We must be knit to Christ, vitally one with Him, just as a branch is really, after a living manner, one with the stem. It would be no use to tie a branch to the stem of the vine; that would not cause it to bring forth fruit. It must be joined to it in a living union, and so we must be joined to Christ in a living union.

We must bear fruit or we will certainly perish.

Do you know, by experience, what that expression means? If you do not know it by experience, you do not know it at all. No one knows what life is except the one who is himself alive, and no one knows what union to Christ is except he who is himself united to Christ. We must become one with Christ by an act of faith; we must be inserted into Him as the graft is placed in the incision made in the tree into which it is to be grafted. Then there must be a knitting of the two together – a vital junction, a union of life, and a flowing of the sap – or else there cannot be any bearing of fruit.

Again, I say, what a serious thing this makes our life to be! How earnest should be our questioning of ourselves! *For the divisions of Reuben there were great searchings of heart* (Judges 5:16), and so there should be about this matter. Let each one of us ask, "Am I bearing fruit? I am not unless I am vitally united to Christ. I have openly professed that I am in Christ, but am I bringing forth fruit unto His honor and glory?"

I think I hear someone say, "I hope I have begun to bring forth some fruit, but it is very little in quantity and it is of very poor quality. I do not suppose that the Lord Jesus will even notice it." Well, now, listen to what the text says; it is the heavenly Bridegroom. It is Christ Himself who speaks to His spouse and invites her to come into the vineyard and look around. For, He says, *the vines with the tender grape give a good smell.*

So, you see, there was some **fruit**, though it could only be spoken of as *the tender grape*. Some read the passage as if the vines in blossom give forth fragrance, while others think it refers to the grape just as it begins to form. It was a poor little thing, but the Lord of the vineyard was the first to notice it. If there is any little fruit unto God upon anyone, our Lord Jesus Christ can see it. Though the berry is barely formed, though it is only like a flower that has just begun to bud, He can see the fruit, and He delights in that fruit.

Another tender grape is **a humble faith in Jesus Christ**. The person might only need to sincerely say, *Lord, I believe; help thou mine unbelief* (Mark 9:24).

Then there comes another tender grape, and that is **a genuine change of life**. The person has evidently turned right around. He is not looking in the direction he used to look, and he is not living as he used to live. At first he fails, and might fail a good many times, like a child who is learning to walk and has many tumbles; but the child will never walk if he does not tumble a bit.

Another very blessed fruit of spiritual life in the soul is **secret devotion**. The person never prayed much before. He sometimes went to a place of worship, but he did not care much about it. Now he tries to get alone for private prayer as often as he can.

What is the Lord's estimate of these tender grapes? What

does He think of that sorrow for sin, that little faith, that humble trust in His atoning sacrifice, that earnest attempt to live a changed life, that weariness of frivolity, that private prayer and study of the Scriptures, that eager desire for more grace, and that childlike love? What does the Lord think of all this?

Well, first, He thinks so much of it that He calls His church to come and look at it. Look at the verses that precede our text: *My beloved spake, and said unto me, Rise up, my love, my fair one, and come away. For, lo, the winter is past, the rain is over and gone; the flowers appear on the earth; the time of the singing of birds is come, and the voice of the turtle is heard in our land; the fig tree putteth forth her green figs* (Song of Solomon 2:10-13).

Then He says, *The vines with the tender grape give a good smell.* Of what do they smell? Well, they smell of **sincerity**. You say, "That young man does not know much, but he is very sincere." I see many people who come to make a confession of their faith in Christ who do not know this or that doctrine or have not had this or that experience, but they are very sincere! I can tell that they are genuine by the way they speak. They often make such dreadful blunders, theologically, that I know they have not learned it by memorization, as they might have done for a lesson. They talk

Our Lord Jesus loves sincerity.

straight out of their loving but ignorant hearts, and I like that they should do so, for it shows how true they are in what they say. Our Lord Jesus loves sincerity. There is no smell as hateful as the smell of hypocrisy. A religious experience that is made to order, religious talk such as some indulge in that is all mere religious jargon, is a stench in the nostrils of God. May the Lord save us from it! But these vines with the tender grape give forth the sweet smell of sincerity.

Next, there is a sweet smell of that which is **heartfelt** about these young believers. Oh, how wholehearted they generally are, how earnest, how lively! Some of the older people eventually talk about the things of God as if they were worn irrelevant and there was nothing of special interest in them, but it is not so with these newborn souls. Everything is bright and fresh and they are lively and full of earnestness, and Jesus loves that kind of spirit.

There is also sure to be about these young Christians the sweet smell of **zeal**, and whatever may be said against zeal, I will fight for it as long as I live. In the work of God, we cannot do without fire. When I see our young men and young women full of zeal for God's glory, I say, "God bless them! Let them go ahead." Some of the old folk want to put a bit in the mouths of these fiery young speeds and reign them in, but I expect that I will always be on their side, saying, "No, let them go as fast as they like. If they have zeal without knowledge, it is better than having knowledge without zeal; only wait a bit, and they will get all the knowledge they need."

These young believers have another sweet smell. They are **teachable**, ready to learn, willing to be taught from the Scriptures and from those whose instructions God blesses to their souls.

There is also another delightful smell about them, and that is that they are generally **very joyful**. While they are singing to the glory of God, some dear old brother who has known the Lord for fifty years is groaning. What is the matter with the good man? I wish that he could catch the sweet contagion of the early joy of those who have just found the Savior. There is something delightful in all joy when it is joy in the Lord, but there is a special brightness about the delight of those who are newly converted.

Some people seem to think that only advanced Christians are worth looking after, but our Lord is not of that opinion. "Oh, it was only a lot of little girls who joined the church," someone said. "A lot of little girls?" That is not the way that our Lord Jesus Christ speaks about His children. He calls them King's daughters, and let them be called so. "They were only a group of boys and young men." Yes, but they are the material of which old men are made, and boys and young men, after all, are of much account in the Master's esteem. May we always have many like this.

Chapter 12

Solely for His Glory

When Jesus understood it, he said unto them, Why trouble ye the woman? for she hath wrought a good work upon me. (Matthew 26:10)

Carefully study the story of the devoted Christian woman who poured the alabaster box of very precious ointment upon the head of our blessed Lord and Savior. Her first and last thoughts were for the Lord Jesus Himself.

Seek to do something for Jesus that will be above all a sacred sacrifice of pure love to Him. Do special and private work for your Lord. Between you and your Lord let there be special manifestations of your love to Him. You might say to me, "What should I do?" I decline to answer. I am not to be a judge for you, especially regarding a private deed of love.

The good woman did not say to Peter, "What should I give?" She did not ask John, "What should I do?" Her heart was inventive. Intercede for your neighbors. Pray for yourselves, but could you not set apart a little time each day in which prayer should be all for the Lord's work? Could you not at such seasons cry with secret pleadings, *Hallowed be thy name. Thy kingdom come, Thy will be done in earth, as it is in heaven* (Matthew 6:9-10)?

Would it not be a wonderful thing at these times to feel that you can go up to your private place of prayer and give your Lord a few minutes of your heart's warmest prayer, that *He shall see of the travail of his soul* (Isaiah 53:11)?

That is one thing that all saints can do. Another holy offering is adoration – the adoring of Jesus. We too often forget this adoration when we meet together, or else we thrust it into a corner. The best part of all our public meetings is the worship – the direct worship – and in this worship, the first place should be given to the worship of the Lord Jesus. Sometimes we sing to edify one another with psalms and hymns, but we should also sing simply and only to glorify Jesus. We are to do this when with others, but should we not also do this when alone? Should not all of us, if we can, find some time in which we will spend time, not in seeking the good of our fellow men or in seeking our own good, but in adoring Jesus, blessing Him, magnifying Him, praising Him, pouring forth our heart's love towards Him, and presenting to Him our soul's reverence and remorse? I suggest this to you, but I cannot teach you how to do it. God's Holy Spirit must show your hearts the way.

I offer you a little counsel now about doing good works for Jesus. Take care that self never creeps in. It is to be all for Jesus. Do not let the repulsive fingers of self-seeking stain your work. Never do anything for Jesus out of love for popularity. Always be glad if your right hand does not know what your left hand does. As much as possible, hide your works from the praise of even your most sensible friend.

At the same time, let me also add that you should never be afraid of any criticism from those who do not know your love for Jesus. This good woman did her work publicly because it was the best way to honor her Lord. If you can honor Him by doing a good work in the marketplace before many others, do not be afraid. To some, the temptation may be to attract public attention; to others, the temptation may be to fear it. Serve your Lord as if no one is watching you, but do not be embarrassed, ashamed, or afraid, even if all the eyes in the universe should gaze upon you. In either case, do not let self come in and defile the service.

Never congratulate yourself after you have worked a work for Jesus. If you say to yourself, "Well done!" you have sacrificed to yourself. Always feel that if you had done all as it should be done, it would still be but your reasonable service. *So likewise ye, when ye shall have done all those things which are commanded you, say, We are unprofitable servants: we have done that which was our duty to do* (Luke 17:10).

Remember that deeds of self-sacrifice are most acceptable to Jesus. He loves His people's gifts when they give and feel that they have actually given. Often we are to measure what we do for Him, not by what we have given, but by what we have left. If we have much left, we have not given as much as that widow who gave two mites. It is certain that we have not, for she gave all her living. Jesus *looked up and saw the rich casting their gifts into the treasury. And he saw also a certain poor widow casting two mites in there. And he said, Of a truth I say unto you that this poor widow has cast in more than they all; for all these have of their abundance cast in unto the offerings of God, but she out of her poverty has cast in all the living that she had* (Luke 21:1-4).

Above all, let us keep out of our heart the thought that is so common in this general life, that nothing is worth doing unless something practical comes out of it. By practical, I mean some obvious result upon the morals or material benefit of others. It is almost universal to ask the question, *Cui bono?* – "What is the good that comes from it? What good will it do to me? What good will it do to my neighbor? To what purpose is this waste?" No, but if it will glorify Christ, do it, and accept that motive as the highest and most conclusive of reasons.

If something you do for Christ should bring you dislike or disapproval and threaten to deprive you of advantages, do it anyway. I consider my own character better than popularity, and worldly gain to be as dust compared with faithfulness to the Lord Jesus. It is the devil's logic that says, "You see, I cannot come out and proclaim the truth because I have a sphere of influence that I keep by compromising with what I fear may be false."

Do what is right and fear not!

Why should we be concerned about it? Do what is right and fear not! The consequences are in God's hand and not yours. If you have done a good work unto Christ, even though it might seem to your poor blurry eyes as if great evil has come from it, yet you have done it. Christ has accepted it and He will mark it down, and in your conscience, He will give you His smile of approval.

There is a good defense for any kind of work that you might do for Jesus, and for Jesus only. However large the cost, nothing is wasted that is used upon the Lord, for Jesus deserves it. What if it did no good for anyone else? Did it please *Him?* He has a right to it. Is nothing to be done for the Master of the feast? Are we to be so long looking after the sheep that we never show honor to the Shepherd? Are the servants to be cared for, and may we do nothing for the well-beloved Lord Himself?

I have sometimes felt in my soul that I wish I had no one to serve except my Lord. When I have tried to do my best to serve God, and a cool-blooded critic has pulled my work to pieces, I have thought, "I did not do it for you! I would not have done it for you! I did it for my Lord. Your judgment is a small matter. You condemn my zeal for truth. You condemn what He commands."

So, you may you go about your service and think, "I do it for Christ, and I believe that He accepts my service. I am well content." Jesus deserves that there should be much done entirely for Him. Do you doubt it? On a father's birthday, a child might bring a present into the house just for him. That present is of no use to the mother or to the children; it cannot be eaten or worn. The father could not give it away to anybody, and it is of no value to anybody but himself. Does anybody say, "What a pity it was to choose such a gift, even though the father is pleased"? No, everybody says, "That is just the thing we like to give to our father, since he must keep it for himself. We intended it to be for him. We had no thought of giving it to anyone else. We are glad that he must use our gift for his own pleasure." So it is with regard to Jesus. Find out what will please Him and do it for Him. Think of no one else in the matter. He deserves all you can do, and infinitely more.

Besides, you may depend upon it that any action that appears useless to you, if you do it out of love for Jesus, has a place in Christ's plan and will be very profitable. The anointing of our Lord's head was said to be useless. "No," said Jesus, "it was done right in its proper place – *she did it for my burial*" (Matthew 26:12).

There have been people who have done heroic deeds for Christ, and at the time they did it they might have asked, "How will this further my Lord's purpose?" But somehow it was the very thing that was needed. When Whitefield and Wesley went out into the fields to preach, it was thought to be a crazy idea, and maybe they would not have attempted it if there had not been an absolute necessity. However, by what seemed to then be a daring deed, they set an example for all England, and open-air preaching has become an accepted method with much benefit.

If you, for Christ s sake, become Quixotic,[13] that is fine; your irrationality may be the wisdom of ages to come.

The loving act of the woman who anointed the head of our Lord was not wasted. It has helped us all down to this very moment. It has remained there in the Book, and all who have read it and are right in heart have been inspired by it to consecrate themselves to serve Jesus out of love for Him. That woman has been proclaiming God's truth for two thousand years. The influence of that alabaster box continues to this day, and it will always be around. Whenever you meet a friend in Europe, Asia, Africa, or America who has done anything for our Lord Jesus, you still smell the perfume of the sacred ointment. Her consecrated act is doing all of us good at this hour; it is filling this house with fragrance.

If you are serving Jesus Christ in your own private way and you do not seek to benefit others as much as to honor Him, it might be that you will be an instructive example to Christians in ages to come. Oh, that I could stir some hearts to a personal consecration to Jesus, my Lord! Young men, we need missionaries to go abroad; are none of you ready to go? Young women, we need those who will look after the sick in the lowest places of our cities; will none of you consecrate yourselves to Jesus, the Savior?

I shook hands with a good missionary of Christ from western Africa. He had been there sixteen years. I believe that they consider four years to be the average time of a missionary's life in that region where malaria is common. He had buried twelve of his companions in his time there. For twelve years, he had scarcely seen the face of a white man. He was going to Africa to live a little while longer, perhaps, but he expected to die soon,

---

13   This is a reference to Don Quixote, a character in Miguel de Cervantes' book by the same title. Quixote was a character with seemingly foolish and impractical ideals and actions. "Quixotic," therefore, means seemingly idealistic, unrealistic, impractical, impossible, etc.

he said. Then he added, as I shook his hand, "Well, many of us may die: perhaps hundreds of us will do so; but Christ will win at the last! Africa will know and will fear our Lord Jesus; and what does it matter what becomes of us – our name, our reputation, our health, our life – if Jesus wins at the last?" What heroic words! What a missionary spirit!

Chapter 13

Fire and A Hammer

Is not my word like as a fire? saith the Lord; and like a hammer that breaketh the rock in pieces? (Jeremiah 23:29)

When the Lord spoke by His servant, Jeremiah, His Word was *like as a fire*. There was something burning about it. Human nature did not like it, but human nature was made to feel its force and power. When the false prophets spoke, they would bow to the people and say all kinds of soft and pleasing things; but when Jeremiah spoke in the name of Jehovah, every word seemed to come down upon his hearers. It was as when a mighty man lifts up a sledgehammer and brings it down with all his force upon the stone he means to break. The message did not comfort the ungodly, but it broke their hearts, for the prophet was seeking, if possible, to separate them from their sins.

The ox knoweth his owner, and the ass his master's crib (Isaiah 1:3), and we are not so foolish that we do not know what truth it is that cheers and comforts our hearts, and what kind of teaching it is that makes us glad in the midst of the winter of our hearts. There is far too much teaching today that will not comfort a mouse. You might hear it to all eternity and never be relieved of a single ounce of the burden of life. You might come in and out of the house of God, and you might perhaps say, "Yes, it is very pretty; but what is that to someone who has the burden of life to carry and the battle of life to fight?"

But when you hear the glorious gospel of the blessed God, it lifts you up out of your discouragements and makes you say, "It is worthwhile to live, it is worthwhile to suffer, and it is worthwhile to press forward, for we see the great love the Lord has toward us and what good things He has laid up in store for those who love Him." The Word of the Lord is like a fire, for it warms and comforts the hearts of His people.

God's Word is *like a hammer that breaketh the rock in pieces.* I do not think that it requires any great education to learn how to use a hammer. It may, but it seems that to use a hammer properly, one has to do nothing but to strike with it. Someone who breaks stones, for example, gets a good strong hammer and a pile of stones to strike at, and he only has to hit them as hard as he can and to keep on hitting them until all are broken.

> Brethren, when you preach, take the gospel hammer and strike as hard as you can with it.

Brethren, when you preach, take the gospel hammer and strike as hard as you can with it. "Oh," you might say, "but I must try to improve the look of my hammer; it must have a mahogany handle!" Never mind about the mahogany handle; use your hammer for striking, for hammers are not for ornament, but they are meant to be used for real hard work.

When you come to use the gospel as it ought to be used, the result is wonderful; it is a rock-breaking thing. "Oh!" you cry, "There is a very stubborn man there!" Strike at him with the gospel. "But he ridicules and scoffs at the truth!" Never mind if he does; keep on hitting him with the gospel. "But in a certain neighborhood, I have swung this hammer against the rock for years, and nothing has come of it!" Still go on swinging it, for this is a hammer that never failed yet. Only continue to use it.

Everything is not accomplished with one stroke, nor, perhaps, with twenty strokes. The rock that does not yield the first time or the second time or the third time or the twentieth time – will yield at last. There is a process of disintegration taking place at every stroke of the hammer. The great mass of rock is inwardly moving, even when you cannot see that it is doing so. There will come at last one blow of the hammer that will seem to accomplish the deed, but all the previous strokes contributed to it and brought the rock into the right state for breaking it up at last.

Hammer away, then, with nothing but the gospel of Jesus Christ. The heart that is struck may not yield even year after year, but it will yield at last.

Now, put the two together – the fire and the hammer – and you will see how God forms His servants who are to be instruments for His use. He puts us into the fire of the Word. He melts, He softens, He subdues us. Then He takes us out of the fire and shapes us with hammer strokes such as only He can give, until He has made us suitable instruments for His use. Then He goes forth to His sacred work of conquering the multitudes, having in His hands the polished instruments that He has forged with the fire and the hammer of His Word.

How often have we seen men who have not been moved even by the law of God, at last won to Christ by the gospel – the gospel of free grace and dying love! It is the gospel of full forgiveness for the greatest sinners, and immediate, irreversible pardon is given in a moment to every sinner who believes in Christ! Oh, how this gospel has acted like a fire and burned up all the sinner's opposition! How this gospel has also been like a hammer to break down human stubbornness!

This is the gospel of redemption through the precious blood

of Jesus. This is the gospel that tells of full atonement made for us. This is the gospel that proclaims that every cent of the ransom price has been paid, and that therefore, whosoever believes in Jesus is free from the law, free from guilt, and free from hell. The proclaiming of this gospel has made men's hearts burn within them, has dashed out the very brains of sin, and has made men joyfully flee to Christ.

So, then, preach the gospel! Proclaim the gospel of justification by faith, the gospel of regeneration by the Holy Spirit, and the gospel of final perseverance through the unchanging love of God. Preach the whole glorious gospel of the blessed God as it is revealed in the covenant of grace, and you will be doing fire-and-hammer work of the very best kind.

As God's Word is like a fire and like a hammer, if we have used it upon ourselves, let us try to use it upon others. I think that there are a great many people in this world whom we give up as hopeless, who have never been really tried and tested with the gospel in all their lives. I am afraid that there are people of whom we speak as unlikely to be converted, who have never been fully brought under the influence of the fire of God's Word or beneath the fall of the hammer of the gospel.

"I brought one person to church," says somebody. I am glad you have; but have you ever spoken faithfully to that person about his soul? "Well, I don't think that I have. I have only spoken a little to him about these things."

Have you ever plainly put the gospel before him? "Well, I do not think he was the type of person to be spoken to in that way." Ah! I see. You thought you were going to burn him without using fire, and to break that rock without lifting the hammer.

The fact is, you believed that something better than the gospel fire was needed in his case, or that something gentler than the gospel hammer was needed. Will you not try that old-fashioned hammer upon him? Will you not try that old fire upon him?

I have heard of congregations where men have said, "No good can be done there." I have wondered what would happen if they were to try preaching one of the old-fashioned kind of gospel sermons. What results would follow if they could get Whitefield to preach or have someone preach the same truth as Whitefield preached?

When I am told that the hearts of the people are not affected by the preaching in any place, I ask, "But was it the gospel with which you tried to affect them? Was it the very Word of God that was preached?" Our words are like paper pellets thrown against the wall; they accomplish nothing. But God's Word is like a shot fired from one of the greatest Woolwich cannons.[14] Where it goes, it crushes through every obstacle and destroys everything that is opposed to it.

> Let it be the same gospel for the children that you give to the adults.

Why should we not always set the whole truth before those whom we seek to save? I believe that sometimes, even in Sunday schools, children are taught "to love gentle Jesus," and so on, as if that were the way of salvation. Why not tell them to believe in the Lord Jesus Christ? Why is love supposed to take the place of faith? Let it be the same gospel for the children that you give to the adults. Give them the same gospel and watch what happens. Let this work be attempted everywhere.

"But," someone says, "there are certain places where you cannot do any good if you try to preach the gospel. You must please the people. You must have amusement and entertainment and sports for them. You must have games and plays and concerts." Very well. Convert sinners that way if you can. I do not object to any method that results in winning souls. Stand on your head if that will save the people; but still, it seems to

---

14   Woolwich was a district in southeast London that was an important military town.

me that if God's Word is like a fire, there is nothing like it for burning its way. If God's Word is like a hammer, there can be nothing like that Word for hammering down everything that stands in the way of Jesus Christ. Why, then, should we not continually try the gospel, and nothing but the gospel?

"Well," someone says, "but the poor people are dirty; we must have various sanitary improvements." Of course we must; get on with that as quickly as you can. The more of such things, the better. There is nothing like soap and paint for dirty people and dirty places, but you may paint and clean them as long as you like, yet that will not save their souls without the gospel of Christ. You can go to them and plead with them about not getting drunk, and I hope you will; the more of it, the better. Make every one of them sober if you can, for it will be a great blessing to them; but still, you have not really done anything permanent if you stop there. Try the gospel! Try the gospel! Try the gospel!

When the gospel was tried against the world in the days of Paul – when the power of the great empire of Rome had crushed out liberty and when lust of the most abominable kind made the world reek in the nostrils of God – nothing was done but preaching Jesus Christ and Him crucified, and the common people heard of Jesus Christ, heard of Him gladly, and believed in Him.

Very soon, down went the false gods and the brutal lusts of the Roman empire, and a great part of the world was filled with the gospel. It will have to be done again, and it must be done again. Remember, though, that it is only to be done by that same Word of the Lord that did it the first time. The sooner we get back to that Word, the better. The more we throw away everything else but the simple proclaiming of that Word, the quicker will be the victory and the more swift and sure will be the triumph for our God and for His Christ.

Chapter 14

Beware of Foxes

Hunt the foxes for us, the little foxes, that spoil the vines. (Song of Solomon 2:15)

Dear young friends who have recently turned to Jesus Christ, there are foxes about. We try all we can to fill in the gaps in the hedge so that we can keep the foxes out, but they are very crafty and they manage to get in sometimes. The foxes in the East are much smaller than ours, and they seem to be even more cunning and more ferocious than those we have in this country, and they do much mischief to the vines.

In the spiritual vineyard there are many kinds of foxes. There is, first, **the one who criticizes everything**. He will spoil the vines if he can, and especially the vines that have the tender grapes. He finds fault with everything that he can see in you who are young believers. You know that you are simply depending upon Christ for salvation, but this person says, "You are no child of God, for you are far from being perfect." If God had no children except those who are perfect, He would have none under heaven.

These overcritical people will find fault with this and that and the other thing in your life and character. You know well enough that you have many imperfections, and if they look for them, they will soon find them. Then they say, "We do not believe that there is any grace at all in you," although you know that by the grace of God you are what you are. It may be that there is a fault in you that they have discovered.

Trust in Christ and do not pay attention to what they say, and you will be delivered from that kind of fox.

Maybe you were taken by surprise and suddenly gave in to sin. They may have even set a trap for you and lured you into it, provoking you to anger and then turning around and saying, "You have made a profession to follow Jesus, have you? That is your type of Christianity, is it?" and so on. May God deliver you from these cruel foxes!

God will often do so by enabling you not to pay attention to them. After all, this is only the way in which all Christians have been tried, and there is nothing strange in your experience from these condemning people. They are not your judges, and you will not be condemned because they condemn you. Go and do your best in the service of your Lord. Trust in Christ and do not pay attention to what they say, and you will be delivered from that kind of fox.

A worse fox even than that one, however, is **the one who flatters**. He comes to you smiling and smirking, and he begins to express his approval of your Christian beliefs and very likely tells you what a fine person you are. Indeed, you are so good that he thinks you are rather too strict and precise in your Christianity and have gone a little over the line! He fully believes in Christianity, he says, although if you watch his life, you will not think so.

He says, though, that he does not want people to be too righteous. He knows that there is a line to be drawn, and he draws it. I could never see where he drew it, but still he says he does, and he thinks that you draw the line a little too near the cross. He says, "You are allowed to be a little more worldly; you cannot get through life very well if you continue as you are. If you do not remain in society, you might as well get out of the world at once. Why do you make yourself appear so superior?"

I know what he is after; he wants to get you back among the ungodly. Satan misses you and wants you back again. He is sending Mr. Flatterer to entice you back, if possible, into your former bondage to himself. Get away from that fox at once! The person who tells you that you are too strict in pursuing holiness ought to be clearly told that you do not want his company.

There never lived a person who was too holy, and there never will live anyone who will imitate Christ too closely or avoid sin too rigidly. Whenever someone says that you are too Puritanical, you can always smell one of these foxes. It would be better if we were all more Puritanical and strict. Has not our Father said to us, *Be ye holy; for I am holy* (1 Peter 1:16)? Did not our Lord Jesus say to His disciples, *Be ye therefore perfect, even as your Father which is in heaven is perfect* (Matthew 5:48)?

Then there comes another fox – **Mr. Worldly Wiseman**.[15] He says, "You are a Christian, but do not be a fool. Carry your religion as far as you can make it benefit you, but if you will lose anything by it, well then, don't you do it. You see, this practice is the custom of the trade. It is not right, I know, but still, other people do it, and you should do it, too. If you don't, you will never succeed in business."

Mr. Worldly Wiseman goes on to say, "It is no big deal if you tell a lie or two or make your advertisements exaggerate things a little bit. Everyone else does it, so why shouldn't you? Then see if you can get a little more out of your customer here and a little more there when he does not know it; it is the custom

---

15   This is from a character in John Bunyan's classic allegory, *Pilgrim's Progress*, also available from Aneko Press.

of the trade. It is the way other people do things, and since it is the custom, of course you must do it."

To all such talk I reply that there is another custom – a custom that God has of turning all liars into hell. Be careful that you do not come under that divine rule and law. There is still another custom that God has – that of cutting down as hypocrites those who do not walk honestly and uprightly towards their fellow men. The plea for what is custom will not stand for a moment at the judgment seat of Christ, and it should carry no weight with us here. I know that there are many young people who, unless they are watchful and careful at the very beginning of their spiritual lives, will become lame and will never walk as they should because this fox has bitten them.

There is another ugly fox about, and that is **the doubting fox**. He comes and says, "You seem very happy and very joyful; but is it true? You appear to have become quite a different person from what you used to be, but is there, after all, such a thing as conversion?" This fox begins nibbling at every doctrine. He even nibbles at your Bible and tries to steal from you this chapter and that verse. May God save you young people from all these foxes!

There are some foxes of **evil doctrine**, and they generally try to ruin our young people. I do not think anybody ever attempts now to convert me from my belief. The other day, when a man was arguing with another person, I asked him, "Why don't you try me?" "Oh," he said, "I have given you up as a bad case. There is no use trying to do anything with you." That is how it is when we get to be thoroughly settled in our convictions of the truth. They give us up, and they generally say that we are such fools that we cannot learn their wisdom, which is quite correct, and we intend to be without their wisdom as long as we live.

With some of the younger people, though, they handle it differently. They say, "Now you are a person of considerable breadth of thought, you have an open mind, and you are a person of culture. It is sad that you cling to those old-fashioned beliefs, which are not really consistent with modern progress." The foolish young fellow thinks that he is great, and so is puffed up with pride.

When a man has to talk about his own culture and when he glories in his own advancement, it is time that we suspected the truth about him. When a man can despise others who are doing much more good than he ever dreamed of doing, and when he can call such people outdated and old-fashioned, it is time that he should get rebuked for his lack of respect, for that is what it really is. These clever men, as far as I know them, are simply covered with a little learning that is not even a thousandth of an inch thick. There is nothing in most of them but mere outward show and ranting.

> First, keep close to Christ, for this is your life; next, keep close to His people, for this is your comfort.

There are some people, though, who hold firmly to the old gospel, who have read as much as these evil foxes are ever likely to do and are fully their equals in learning, though they do not care to boast of their accomplishments. I do not want any of you young people to be carried away with the opinion that all educated people are heretics. It is often the reverse, and it is your pretending, shallow philosopher who goes running after heresy. Get out of the way of that fox, or else he will do much damage to the tender grapes.

If you have any sign of spiritual life, if you have any tender grapes upon your branches, the devil and his foxes will be sure to be after you. Therefore, strive to get as close as you can to two people who are mentioned steadily in my text – namely, the King and His spouse. First, keep close to Christ, for this is your life; next, keep close to His people, for this is your comfort. Get among elderly Christian people and seek to learn from those who have long known the Lord. Learn to live for God from those who are farther along the heavenly road than you are.

Pilgrims to Zion should go to heaven in company, and often, when they go in company and they can get a Mr. Greatheart to go before them, it saves them from many Giant Slaygoods and many Giant Grims, and they have a safe and happy journey to the Celestial City, where otherwise they might have been oppressed and worried.

Keep close to God's people, whoever they may be; they are the best company for you, young believers. Some Christians may, like Bunyan's Pilgrim, start on the road to heaven alone; but they miss much comfort that they might have had with companions of a kindred spirit. As for Christiana and her children, and the younger people especially, they will do well to travel with one of the Lord's champions and with the rest of the soldiers of the Lord carrying banners who are marching toward the Celestial City.[16]

---

16   As with Mr. Worldly Wiseman earlier, Pilgrim, Mr. Greatheart, Giant Slaygood, Giant Grim, Christiana, and the Celestial City are all names of people or places from John Bunyan's *Pilgrim's Progress*. Charles Spurgeon loved that book. He said, "Next to the Bible, the book I value most is John Bunyan's *Pilgrim's Progress*. I believe I have read it through at least a hundred times. It is a volume of which I never seem to tire; and the secret of its freshness is that it is so largely compiled from the Scriptures."

Chapter 15

Good Things Take Time

My doctrine shall drop as the rain, my speech
shall distil as the dew, as the small rain upon the
tender herb, and as the showers upon the grass.
(Deuteronomy 32:2)

We are all to be teachers of the gospel according to our
ability, and the way to do it is to be *as the small rain
upon the tender herb.* Maybe you say, "Well, I would be small
rain without any great effort, for I do not have much in me."
Maybe so, but that small rain has a way of its own by which it
makes up for being so small.

How does it do that, you ask? It does so by continuing to
fall day after day. Any gardener will tell you that there is more
done with many hours of gentle rain than in a short period with
a drenching shower. Constant dropping penetrates, saturates,
and abides.

Little deeds of kindness win love even more certainly than
one big good-hearted act. If you cannot say much gospel truth
at a time, keep on saying a little and saying it often. If you cannot come out with a truckload of grain for an army, feed the
barndoor fowls with a handful at a time. If you cannot give the

people fulness of doctrine like the profound preachers of former ages, you can at least tell others what the Lord has taught you, and then ask Him to teach you more.

As you learn, teach; as you get, give; as you receive, distribute. Be as the gentle rain upon the tender herb. Don't you think that in trying to bring people to Christ we sometimes try to do too much at once? Rome was not built in a day, nor will a neighborhood be saved in a week. People do not always receive all the gospel the first time they hear it.

To break hearts for Jesus is something like splitting wood; we need to work with wedges that are very small at one end, but increase in size as they are driven in. A few sentences spoken well and appropriately may leave an impression where the attempt to force conversion at once upon a person may provoke resistance and do harm. Be content to drop a word or two today and another word or two tomorrow. Soon you may safely say twice as much, and in a week's time you may hold a long distinctly religious conversation. It may soon happen that where the door was rudely shut in your face, you will become a welcome visitor, whereas if you had forced your way in at first, you would have effectually destroyed all future opportunity.

There is much benefit in speaking at the right moment. We may show our wisdom in *not* doing and in *not* saying, as much as in doing and saying. Time is a great ingredient in success. To speak out of season will show our zeal, but not always our sense. *Preach the word; be instant in season, out of season; reprove, rebuke, exhort with all long suffering and doctrine* (2 Timothy 4:2). We are to be instant out of season as well as in season, but this does not involve incessant talking.

I suggest to all who desire to be winners of souls by personal effort to be *as the small rain upon the tender herb.* The rain is seasonable and is in accordance with its surroundings. The rain does not fall while a burning sun is scorching the plants, or it might kill them; neither is the rain always falling, or it might injure them. Do not bring in your exhortations when they would be out of place, and do not be incessantly talking even the best of truth, lest you weary with rambling those whom you desire to convince with argument. If you will wait upon the Lord for guidance, He will send you forth when you will be most useful, even as He does the rain. God will direct you as to time and place if you put yourself at His disposal.

Gentle rain is meant to enter the herb so that it can drink in the nourishment and be truly refreshed. The rain is not to drench the herb or flood it, but is to feed it, to revive it, to refresh it. This was what Moses aimed at. This is what all true preachers of Christ aim at. We desire that the word that we speak may enter into the souls of those listening, that it will be taken up into the innermost nature and will produce its own divine result.

> Gentle rain is meant to enter the herb so that it can drink in the nourishment and be truly refreshed.

Why is it that some people never seem to appreciate the concept of *the small rain upon the tender herb*? I suppose it is, first, because some of it may be above their understanding. If you hear a sermon and you do not know at all what the preacher is talking about, how can it benefit you? If the preacher uses the high-class pulpit language of the day, full of theological and scholarly terms and Greek and Hebrew words, then the hearer usually wastes his time, and the preacher has wasted his labor.

One person said to me, "If I went to such-and-such a church I would not need my Bible, but I would need a dictionary, for otherwise I would not know what was meant." May that never be the case with us! When people cannot understand the meaning of our language, how can we expect that they can drink in the inner sense?

We cannot feed upon that which is high above and out of our

sight. Progressing in theology is all very fine, but it is of no use to poor souls down here below who cannot understand these terms. Tender plants are not refreshed by water that is carried up in the clouds, but they need it to come down to earth and moisten their leaves and roots. If it does not come near them, how can they be refreshed by it? The fountains of Versailles are very grand, but for the little flowerpot in a window, a cupful from a child's hand poured near the root will suffice.

As the small rain upon the tender herb. Now observe that in looking around among mankind, whenever wise people expect any result from their labors, they always go to work in a manner suited and adapted to the end they have in view. If Moses wants his speech to bless those whom he compares to tender herbs, he makes it like small rain. I see clearly that he seeks a result, for he adapts his means.

There is a kind of trying to do good that I call the hit-or-miss style. With this style, you intend to do good, but you do not consider what method of doing good you are best suited for. You might want to preach, and so you preach. Of course, you must give a sermon, and so you give a sermon. There is no consideration about the congregation and its spiritual needs or what truth will be most likely to convict and benefit. Hit or miss, off you go!

When a man intends to see results, he begins studying methods and their adaptation to ends. If he sees that his people are strong men and he wants to feed them, he does not bring out the milk jug, but he brings out a plate of good meat for them. You can see that he intends to feed his people, for he has great concern when preparing their spiritual meat. When a person wants to water plants, and they are tender herbs, he does not drench them if he wants good results. That would look as if he had no real purpose but was simply going through a routine. Moses meant what he was doing. Finding the people to be comparable to tender herbs, he adapted his speech to them and made it like the small rain.

What will be the result if we do the same? It will happen that there will be among us young converts like tender herbs, newly planted, and if we speak in tenderness and gentleness we will see the result, for they will take root in the truth and grow in it. Paul planted, and then Apollos watered. *I have planted, Apollos watered, but God gave the increase* (1 Corinthians 3:6). Why did Apollos water? Because you must water plants after you have planted them so that their roots can grow more deeply.

> You must water plants after you have planted them so that their roots can grow more deeply.

How happy you will be if you use your advanced experience to strengthen those whose new life is yet weak! You will have loving honor as tender fathers, and your wise advice will be *as the small rain upon the tender herb,* for you will see the result in the young people taking hold of Christ and drinking up the precious nutrients stored away in the soil of God's Word that they may grow thereby. *As newborn babes, desire the sincere milk of the word, that ye may grow thereby* (1 Peter 2:2).

When your speech is like small rain to the tender herb, the weak and perishing revive and lift up the head. The herb was withering at first. It was leaning over as you see a newly planted thing do, weak and ready to die; but the small rain came, and it seemed to say, "Thank you," and it looked up, lifted its head, and recovered from its weakness.

You will see a reviving effect produced upon spiritually weak hearts and discouraged minds. You will be a comforter, you will inspire away the fears of many, and you will make glad the timid and fearful. What a blessing it is when you see that result, for then there is so much more joy in the world, and God is so much more glorified!

When you water tender herbs and see them grow, you have a further reward. It is delightful to watch the development and increase of grace in those who are under our care. This has been an exceedingly sweet pleasure to me. I use my own experience as an example, because I have no doubt it is repeated in many of you. It has been a great delight to me to meet men serving God and preaching the gospel gloriously who were once young converts and in need of my fostering care. I know men, deacons of churches, fathers in Israel, that I remember talking to twenty or twenty-five years ago, when they could not speak a word for Jesus, for they were not assured of their own salvation. I rejoice to see them now leaders of the flock, whereas once they were poor, feeble lambs. I carried them in my bosom, and now they might almost carry me. I am glad enough to learn from them and sit at their feet.

We water plants so that we can see them bring forth fruit and become prepared for use. So we will see those whom God blesses by our means become a joy to the Lord Himself, yielding fruits of holiness, patience, and obedience such as Jesus Christ delights in. His joy is in His people, and when He can rejoice in them, their joy is full.

Let us try to be little in our own esteem so that we can be as the small rain. Let us try to be a little useful if we cannot reach to great things. The small rain is a great blessing. Let us try to be useful in little things. Let us look after tender herbs; let us try to bring boys and girls to Jesus. Let us look after the tender plants of the Lord's right-hand planting – those who are babes in grace – the timid, trembling, half-hoping, half-fearing ones.

Chapter 16

The Urgency of Today

*Then they said one to another, We do not well: this
day is a day of good tidings, and we hold our peace:
if we tarry till the morning light, some mischief will
come upon us: now therefore come, that we may go
and tell the king's household.* (2 Kings 7:9)

God had visited the Syrian camp and had by Himself alone
defeated the entire Syrian army. Every single Syrian
soldier had fled. Though the starving citizens of Samaria did
not know it, the Lord had made provision in abundance for all
their hunger, and there it was, within a stone's throw of the city
gates. The Lord had done it. His own right hand and His holy
arm had gotten Him the victory. He had provided for Israel's
needs, though they did not know it. These lepers found out
the joyful facts and had utilized their discovery by entering
into possession of the treasure. They were appointed to make
the joyful facts known, and if they had concealed them, they
would have been guilty men.

No person has done all the good he could have done and
should have done. If anyone assures me that he has done all
the good that had been possible for him to do, I do not believe

him. I will say no more about that, but let us labor to avoid sins of omission. If you know the Lord and have never confessed His name, then you have not done well. If you have been in a group of people and have not spoken up for Christ, you have not done well. If you have had opportunities of telling others, even children, the gospel, and you have not done so, you have not done well.

It is a serious accusation, after all, for a person's conscience to bring against him when it forces him to join with others in saying, *We do not well.* That is the reason why the barren fig tree was cut down. He who kept the vineyard did not say, "Cut it down, for it bears such sour fruit." It bore no fruit at all. There was the point: it simply took up room and was not doing what it was supposed to do.

Had those lepers held their tongues, they would actually have been doing evil. Suppose that they had kept their secret for twenty-four hours and many hundreds had died of starvation within the walls of Samaria. If they had so perished, would not the lepers have been guilty of their blood? Do you not agree with that? Cannot neglect be murder just as truly as a stab or a shot?

If, in your neighborhood, a person perishes through not knowing the Savior, and you never made an effort to instruct him, how will you be guiltless at the last great day? If there is anyone within your reach who sinks down to eternal destruction because he lacked the knowledge of Christ when you could have given him that knowledge, will you be free from his blood in the day when the great examination will be held and God will make inquiry for the blood of all people?

Cannot neglect be murder just as truly as a stab or a shot?

These lepers, if they had remained silent, would have acted most improperly. Notice how they put it themselves. They said, *We do not well: this day is a day of good tidings, and we hold our peace.* Has Jesus washed your sins away, and are you silent about it?

I remember the day when I first found peace with God through the precious blood. I just had to tell somebody about it. I could not have silenced the voice within me. Are you saved in the Lord with an everlasting salvation, and can you keep the blessing to yourself? Do you not wonder that all the timbers in your house do not groan at you, and that the earth itself does not open her mouth to rebuke you? Can you be such an ungrateful wretch as to have tasted of God's amazing mercy and yet have no word to say by way of declaring it to others?

Overcome that timid spirit. Cry out, "I cannot help it; I am driven to it. I must and will bear witness that there is a Savior, and a great one." Personally, I cannot hold my tongue, and I never will while I can speak.

> E'er since by faith I saw the stream,
>   Thy flowing wounds supply;
> Redeeming love has been my theme,
>   And shall be till I die![17]

The church of God has a claim upon all of you who have discovered the great love of Jesus. Come and tell your fellow Christians. Tell the good news to the King's household. The church of God is often greatly refreshed by the stories of new converts. I am afraid that we who get over fifty years old come by degrees to be rather fossilized, and it is a great blessing to us to hear the cries of the babes in grace and to listen to the fresh and vivid testimony of new converts. It stirs our blood and quickens our souls, and thus the church of God is benefited.

Besides that, a decided testimony for Christ is due to the

---

17   From "There is a Fountain," a hymn by William Cowper (1731-1800).

world. If a man is a soldier of the cross and does not show his colors and reveal which side he is on, all his colleagues lose by his lack of decision. There is nothing better for a man when he is brought to Christ than for him to clearly express his faith and let those around him know that he is a new man. Fly your flag of loyalty. Taking a stand to live for Christ and holiness will save you from many dangers and will repel many temptations. Compromise creates a life of misery.

If all Christians came out and boldly declared what the Lord has done for their souls, the world would feel the power of Christianity. The world would not think of it as they now do, as though it were some small-minded superstition of which its own supporters were ashamed. If indeed you are soldiers of the cross, carry your shields into the light of day and do not be ashamed of your Captain! What can there be to make us ashamed in the service of such a Lord? Be ashamed of shame, and act like men (see 1 Samuel 4:9)! If you are a soldier in the army of the Lord, then stand and fight bravely!

You owe your open confession of allegiance to Jesus Christ to all others, and especially to yourself. It is due to your spiritual maturity that, if the Lord has done anything for you, you should gratefully acknowledge it. You are also obligated because of your love for others – and love of others is the very essence of Christianity – that you should plainly declare that you are on the Lord's side. *Then Moses stood in the gate of the camp, and said, Who is on the Lord's side?* (Exodus 32:26). What more should I say? What more do I need to say? I desire to sound the trumpet and call to our Lord's banner all Christians who are good and true.

This declaration should be continually made. I speak here of many who have confessed Christ publicly and are not ashamed of His name. We should always make Christ known, not only by our once-made profession of faith when we first were born

again, but by frequently bearing witness in support of that profession. I wish that we did this more among God's own people.

Miss Havergal[18] very admirably says, "The king's household
were the most unlikely people to need to be instructed in this
good news – so it seems at first sight. But, secondly, the lepers
were the most unlikely persons to instruct the king's household;
and yet they did so."

You and I might say, "Christian people do not need to be
spoken to about our Lord and His work; they know more than
we do. If they do need it, who are we, who are less than the
least of all our Master's household, that we should presume to
instruct them?" Thus, even humility might prevent us from
bearing our testimony among certain groups of people.

If you were in the middle of a group of people ignorant of
Christ to whom you could do good, you might feel obligated to
speak; but among Christians you are likely to be silent. Have
you not said to yourself, "I could not speak to that good old
man. He is much better instructed in the faith than I am"?
Meanwhile, what do you think that good old man is saying? He
says to himself, "He is a fine young man, but I could not speak
to him, for he has so much more ability than I have." Thus you
are both as mute as mice when you could be mutually edified.

Worse still, perhaps you begin talking about worthless topics
such as the weather, the latest scandal, or politics. Suppose we
were to change all this, and each man says, "I am a Christian
man, and the next time I meet a brother Christian, whether
he is older and wiser or not, I will speak to him of our common Master."

If two children meet, they do well to speak of their father
and mother. If one is a very little child, he may only know
a little about his father compared with the knowledge possessed by his big sister, but maybe he has kissed his father last

---

18   Frances Ridley Havergal (1836-1879), English poet and hymn writer.

and has enjoyed more expression of love from his father lately than his grown-up sister has. The older can tell more of her father's wisdom and providence, but the younger has a more vivid sense of his tenderness and love; and so they can unite in fervent admiration.

Why should Christian people so often meet and part without exchanging five words about the Lord Jesus? I am not condemning any of you, for I am rebuking myself more than anyone else. We do not bear enough testimony for our Lord. I was quite startled the other day when a theater worker said to me, "You believe that the Lord directs the way of His people, don't you, sir?" I said, "That I do. Do you know anything about it?" "Why," he said, "yes. This morning I was praying to the Lord to direct my way, and now you are speaking with me. I felt that it was a good beginning for the day."

We began talking about the things of God directly. That man should not have been the first to speak about God; as a minister of the gospel, I should have spoken to him about the Lord. We have much to blame ourselves for in this respect. We neglect to say something because we don't know how a word might be received, but we might as well try. No harm can come from trying.

Suppose you were to go into a place where people were sick and dying, and you had medicine that would heal them. Would you not be eager to give them some of it? Would you say nothing about it because you were not sure how it might be received? How could you know how it would be received except by making the offer? Tell poor souls about Jesus. Tell them how His grace healed you, and maybe they will answer, "You are the very person I need; you have brought me the news I have desired to hear."

There are districts in London, to my knowledge, in the suburbs especially, where, if a man knocks at the door and begins to speak about Christ, the poor people answer, "No one ever calls upon us to do us any good. We are left to perish." It is shameful that it should be so, but so it is.

People live and die in this Christian country as much lost to the knowledge of the gospel as if they had lived on the Congo. If they lived on the Congo, we would all donate to send a missionary up the river to tell them about Jesus and His love. Even at the risk of his dying of fever, we would send a missionary to them, and yet those who live next door to us or those with whom we work are left in ignorance of salvation.

> It is not enough to me that I myself preach the gospel, but I want to motivate others to proclaim it, too.

The woman who works in the factory, the man who cleans the building – these people may know no more of Christ than the unreached people in foreign lands, yet we do not speak about Christ to them. Is this not shocking? We have satisfied our own hunger, and now we allow others to starve! Let us stop our lack of concern and get to work for Jesus. It is not enough to me that I myself preach the gospel, but I want to motivate others to proclaim it, too.

I once spoke about some Christian young men who were great at a certain sport, but could not talk straight at a sinner's heart. A gentleman who heard me said, "That is true about me. I am a Christian man, but I am better known as an athlete than as a Christian worker." He began to serve his Lord with his whole heart, and today he is being greatly used by God. Oh, that I could win others to be this way! The multitudes around us are dying in the dark. I beg you to take them all the light you have! Millions are perishing all over this land. Hurry to their rescue! The world remains under the power of evil. I urge you to reclaim it!

"I don't know much," someone says. Then don't say what you don't know.

"Oh!" cries another, "I hope I am a Christian." Tell others how you became a believer, and that will be the gospel. You do not need to study a book and try to make a sermon with three heads and a tail. Simply go home and say to your oldest son, "John, I want to tell you how your father found a Savior." Go home to that sweet little daughter of yours and say, "Dear Sarah, I want to tell you how Jesus loves me." Before the morning light you may have the joy of seeing your dear children brought to the Savior – if this very evening you talk to them out of the fullness of your heart.

Chapter 17

Open Your Mouth

Therefore they that were scattered abroad went every where preaching the word. Then Philip went down to the city of Samaria, and preached Christ unto them. . . . Then Philip opened his mouth, and began at the same scripture, and preached unto him Jesus.
(Acts 8:4-5, 35)

I n every church where there really is the power of the Spirit of God, the Lord will cause it to be spread abroad, more or less. He never intends that a church should be like a nut shut up in a shell or like ointment enclosed in a box. The precious perfume of the gospel must be poured forth to sweeten the air.

Right now in this land we do not have much of that kind of persecution that drives people from their homes, but godly people are scattered about through the necessity of earning a living. Sometimes we regret that certain young men have to move quite a distance for their work, but should we regret it? We lament that certain families must move across the country or even across the world, but does not the Lord by this means sow the good seed widely?

It is very pleasant to be comfortably settled under an edifying ministry, but the Lord has need of some of His servants in places where there is no light. In many ways the great Head of the church scatters His servants abroad, but they ought of themselves to scatter voluntarily. Every Christian should ask, "Where can I do the most good?" and if he can do more good anywhere beneath the sun than in the land of his birth, he ought to go there, if he can. God wants His people scattered around the world, and if we will not go willingly, He may use providential necessity as the forcible means of moving us.

> Every converted man is to teach what he knows to be true.

The Lord's design is not to scatter us just to scatter His people, but He scatters for a purpose. He intended that, being scattered, the saints of Jerusalem should go everywhere preaching the Word.

I would call your attention to the translation in the Revised Version, where Philip is said to have *proclaimed* the Word. The word *proclaim* is not quite so subject to the modern sense which has spoiled the word "preach." *Preach* has come to be a sort of official term for delivering a set discourse, whereas gospel preaching is talking, discoursing, and sharing the gospel truth in any way. We are to make known the Word of the Lord.

Every converted man is to teach what he knows to be true. All those who have drunk of the living water are to become fountains out of which shall flow rivers of living water. *He that believeth on me, as the scripture hath said, out of his belly shall flow rivers of living water* (John 7:38). We will never get back to the grand old times of spiritual conquest until we get back to the old method of being fully devoted. In proportion as we come as Christians to individual service – nobody dreaming of doing his work by letting someone else do the work for him, but each one serving God for himself – in that proportion, under the blessing of God, we will come back to the old success.

There were no professional exceptions. Philip is mentioned as going down to Samaria to preach, but Philip was originally set apart to attend the distribution of charity of the church. It is good for every man to attend to his own special duty, but where that duty ceases to be needful, let him get to that work that is common and constant.

The time may come when you no longer have need for the specific duties of a specific deacon. What does the deacon do? As the work to which he was appointed has come to an end, he keeps to the work for which every Christian is appointed, and he proclaims the gospel of Jesus Christ. None of us, then, can be exempted from the work of preaching the gospel because we are engaged in some other work.

As good as it is, though it may be very intimately connected with the kingdom of Christ, yet it does not excuse us from the work of trying to bring sinners to Christ in some way or other. Stephen, the deacon, began first to bear testimony, and when he died, Philip, the next on the list, stepped into his place. One soldier falls and another steps forward. All of us are to proclaim the Word, and no one is exempted by another form of service. Oh, that the Lord's people everywhere would be mindful of this!

There were no educational or literary exceptions. It is thought nowadays that a man must not try to proclaim the gospel unless he has had a good education. To preach Christ while committing grammatical errors is looked upon as a serious offense. People are greatly offended at the idea of the gospel being properly preached by an uneducated man. I believe this to be a very damaging mistake. There is nothing whatsoever in the whole range of Scripture to excuse any mouth from speaking for Jesus when the heart is truly acquainted with His salvation.

We are not all called to "preach" in today's sense of the term, but we are all called to make Jesus known if we know Him. Has the gospel ever been preached to any extent by men of high literary power? Look through the whole line of history and see if it is so. Have the men of splendid eloquence been notable for winning souls? I could quote names of those who are among the greatest orators who are not effective at all as soul winners.

Those whom God has most honored have been men who, whatever their gifts, have consecrated them to God and have earnestly declared the great truths of God's Word. Men who have been thoroughly in earnest and have faithfully described man's ruin by sin and God's remedy of grace – men who have warned sinners to escape from the wrath to come by believing in the Lord Jesus – these men have been useful. If they had great gifts, they were not damaging to them; if they had few talents, this did not disqualify them.

It has pleased God to use the lowly things of this world and things that are despised for the accomplishment of His great purposes of love. Paul declared that he did not proclaim the gospel with wisdom of words. He said, *Christ sent me . . . to preach the gospel: not with wisdom of words, lest the cross of Christ should be made of none effect* (1 Corinthians 1:17). He feared what might happen if he used fine rhetoric, and therefore he refused the wisdom of words. We have need to do so now with emphasis. Let us trust in the divine power of the Holy Spirit and speak the truth in reliance upon His might, whether we can speak fluently with Apollos (Acts 18:24), or are slow of speech like Moses (Exodus 4:10).

Our Lord intends to bring in the rest of His chosen through those who are already called, but if these people do not tell others and are untrue to their calling, how is the work to be done? I know the work is of God alone, but He uses human instruments. If you do not tell the gospel, you are letting others perish.

The main reason that the early church constantly proclaimed Jesus was that they were in a fine state of spiritual health. They went everywhere preaching the Word when scattered abroad because they had done the same when at home. You will never make a missionary of the person who does no good at home. If you do not seek souls in your own street, you will not do so in another country on the other side of the world. If you are of no use in your hometown, you will be of no use on another continent. He who will not serve the Lord in the Sunday school at home will not win children to Christ in China. Distance lends no real charm to Christian service.

You who do nothing now are not fit for the war, for you are in sad health. However, if the Lord gives you spiritual health and vigor, then you will not need to be urged on, but you will cry at once, "Here am I; send me!" *I heard the voice of the Lord saying, Whom shall I send, and who will go for us? Then I answered, Here am I; send me* (Isaiah 6:8).

Chapter 18

God's Limitless Providence

A great multitude followed him, because they saw
his miracles which he did on them that were dis-
eased. (John 6:2)

L ook – there are the people! There are five thousand of them,
as hungry as hunters, and they all need to have food given
to them, for none of them can travel to buy it! And here is the
provision: five thin wafers – and those of barley, more fit for
horses than for men – and two little fish. Five thousand people
and a few biscuits and fish wherewith to feed them! The dis-
proportion is enormous; if each person would receive only the
tiniest crumb, there still would not be enough for all.

In like manner, there are thousands of people in our towns,
and only a handful of wholehearted Christians earnestly desir-
ing to see them converted to Christ. There are billions of people
in this round world, and oh, so few missionaries breaking to
them the bread of life. It is almost as few for the billions as were
these five barley cakes for those five thousand!

The problem is a very difficult one. The contrast between
the supply and the demand would have struck us much more
vividly if we had been there in that crowd at Bethsaida than

it does here, two thousand years afterward, merely hearing about it. But the Lord Jesus was equal to the emergency. None of the people went away without sharing in His bounty; they were all filled.

Our blessed Master, now that He has ascended into the heavens, has more rather than less power. He is not mystified because of our lack, but can even now use meager means to accomplish His own glorious purposes. Therefore, let no one's heart fail him. Do not despair of the evangelization of this city, nor think it hopeless that the gospel should be preached in all nations for a testimony unto them. Have faith in God, who is in Christ Jesus. Have faith in the compassion of the Great Mediator. He will not desert the people in their spiritual need any more than He failed that hungry crowd in their earthly need long ago.

Notice the providence of God in bringing the boy there. We do not know his name. We are not told anything concerning his family. Was he a little peddler who thought that he could make some money by selling a few loaves and fish, and had he nearly sold out? Was he a boy whom the apostles had employed to carry this tiny provision for the use of Jesus and His friends? We do not know much about him, but he was the right boy in the right place that day. Whatever his name might have been, it did not matter; he had the barley loaves and the fish upon which the people were to be fed.

Christ is never in need that He does not have someone there to meet that need. Have faith in the providence of God. I do not know what made the boy bring the loaves and fish, but bring them he did. Boys often do unexplainable things. God, who understands the ideas and motives of boys and who takes into account even barley loaves and fish, had appointed that boy to be there. Again I say, believe in the providence of God.

Mr. Stanley[19] tells us that when he came out of his long journey through the forest, I think after a hundred and sixty days of walking in darkness, and found himself at last where he could see the sun, he felt that there was a special providence of God that had taken care of him. I am very glad that Mr. Stanley felt that it was the hand of God that had brought him out of the displeasing shade, but I do not need to go to Africa to learn that we are surrounded by God's goodness.

Many of us have felt a special providence of God in our own homes. We have met with His hand in connection with our own children. Every day we are surrounded by signs of His care. *Whoso is wise, and will observe these things, even they shall understand the lovingkindness of the Lord* (Psalm 107:43). "I am sure God took care of me," someone said, "for as I was walking along

> He will never desert His people.

a certain street, I slipped on a piece of orange peel and had what might have been a serious fall, yet I was not hurt in the least." His friend replied, "I am sure God has taken care of me, for I have walked along that street hundreds of times and have never slipped on a piece of orange peel or on anything else."

Let us also believe in His providence with regard to the church of Christ. He will never desert His people. He will find men when He needs them. It has always been this way throughout the history of the saints, and it will always be this way.

Before the Reformation there were many educated men who knew something of Christ's gospel, but they said it was a pity to make a lot of noise, so they communed with one another and with Christ very quietly. What was needed was some rough bullheaded fellow who would blurt the gospel out and upset the old state of things. Where could he be found?

---

19   Sir Henry Stanley (1841-1904) was a Welsh reporter and explorer famous for exploring Africa in search of missionary David Livingstone.

There was a monk named Luther who, while he was reading his Bible, suddenly stumbled on the doctrine of justification by faith. He was the man needed at that time. However, when he went to a dear brother in the Lord and told him how he felt, his friend said to him, "Go back to your room and pray and commune with God, and hold your tongue." But then, you see, he had a tongue that he could not hold – and that nobody else could hold – and he began to use it to speak the truth that had made a new man of him.

The God who made Martin Luther knew what He was doing when He made him. God put within Luther a great burning fire that could not be restrained, and it burst forth and set the nations on fire. Never despair about providence. There sits tonight, somewhere in a quiet corner in the country, a man who will turn the current of unbelief and win back the churches to the old gospel. *Thus saith the Lord, Stand ye in the ways, and see, and ask for the old paths, where is the good way, and walk therein, and ye shall find rest for your souls* (Jeremiah 6:16).

There never yet was a point of distress as to God's truth when someone did not suddenly come forward – a David with a sling and a stone, a Samson with a jawbone, or a Shamgar with an ox goad – who defeated the adversaries of the Lord. *There is a lad here.* The providence of God had sent him. *There is a lad here, who has five barley loaves and two small fishes, but what are they among so many?* (John 6:9). This lad with his loaves was brought to the forefront. When they were searching for all the provisions in the crowd, this unknown boy who never would have been heard of elsewhere was brought to the front because he had his little basket of biscuits. Andrew found him out, and he went to Jesus and said, *There is a lad here, who has five barley loaves and two small fishes.*

Rest assured that if you have the Bread of Life about you and you are willing to serve God, you do not need to be afraid that not being well-known will ever prevent you from serving God. "Nobody knows me," someone says. Well, it is not a very desirable thing that everyone should know you. Those of us who are known to everyone would be very glad if we were not; there is no great comfort in it. He who can work away for his Master with nobody to see him but his Master is the happiest of men.

"I only have one hundred people to preach to," a country pastor said to me. I replied, "If you give a good account of those hundred, you have quite enough to do." If all you have is very little – just that small amount of loaves and fish – use it properly, and you will serve your Master well. In due time, when God wants you, He knows where to find you. You do not need to put an advertisement in the newspaper. He knows the street you live on and the number on the door.

> He who can work away for his Master with nobody to see him but his Master is the happiest of men.

You do not need to go and push yourself to the front. The Lord will bring you to the front when He wants you, and I hope that you do not want to get there if He does not want you there. You can depend upon it, that if you push your way forward when you are not required, God will put you back again. Oh, for grace to work on unobserved, to have your one talent, your five loaves and two fish, and only to be noticed when the hour suggests the need and the need makes a loud call for you.

When they were noticed, the loaves and fish did not seem to do very well; they were judged insufficient for the purpose. Andrew asked, *What are they among so many?* The boy's candle seemed to be quite snuffed out. What could be the use of something so insignificant?

Some of you have had Satan asking you, "What is the use of your trying to do anything?" To you, dear mother, with a family of children, he has whispered, "You cannot serve God."

He knows very well that, by sustaining grace, you can indeed serve God, and he is afraid of how well you can serve God if you bring up those dear children in His fear. He says to the sincere individual over there, "You do not have much ability; what can you do?" Ah, dear friend! He is afraid of what you can do, and if you will only do what you can do, God will, before long, help you to do what now you cannot do. The devil is afraid of even the little that you can do now, and many children of God seem to side with Satan in despising the day of small things. *Who hath despised the day of small things?* (Zechariah 4:10).

What are they among so many? So few, so poor, so lacking in talent – what can any of us hope to do? Looked down upon, even by the disciples, it is no wonder if we are looked down upon by the world. The things that God will honor, man must first despise. You face and endure the derision of those of the world, and afterward you come out to be used of God.

Though seemingly inadequate to feed the multitude, the loaves and fish would have been quite enough for the boy's supper, yet he seems to have been quite willing to part with them. The disciples would not have taken them from him by force; the Master would not have allowed it. The boy willingly gave them up to be the start of the great feast. Somebody might have said to the boy, "John, you know that you will soon be able to eat that bread and those two little fish; keep them for yourself. Get away into a corner; every man for himself."

Is it not a good rule to "take care of number one"? Perhaps, but the boy whom God uses will not be selfish. I may be speaking to some young Christian to whom Satan says, "Make money first and serve God later. Stick to business and succeed; then, after you become successful, you can live more like a Christian and give some money away." Let such a person remember the barley loaves and the fish.

If that boy had really wisely considered what was for his own good instead of merely yielding with a generous impulse to the demand of Christ, he still would have done exactly what he did. He would have realized that if he had kept the loaves, he would have eaten them and they would have been gone; but now that he brought them to Christ, all those thousands of people got fed, and he gets as much himself as he would have had if he had eaten his own food. In addition, he gets a share out of the twelve baskets full of fragments that remain.

Anything that you take away from self and give to Christ is well invested. It will often bring in ten thousand percent. The Lord knows how to give such a reward to an unselfish person so that he will feel that he who saves his life loses it, but he who is willing even to lose his life and the bread that sustains it is the one who, after all, truly gets saved.

This, then, is the history of these loaves. They were sent there through God's providence by a boy who was sought out and noticed. What he had brought was despised, but he was willing to give it, whether it was despised or not. He would yield it to his Lord. Do you see what I am driving at? I want to get the attention of some of these boys and girls and young men and young women. I will not bother about your age; you can be called boys if you are under seventy. I

> **Anything that you take away from self and give to Christ is well invested.**

want to get hold of you who think that you have very little ability, and I want to say to you, "Come and bring it to Jesus." We need you. Times are hard. The people are famishing. Though nobody appears to need you, yet be courageous and do what you can. Who knows but that, like Queen Esther, you may have *come to the kingdom for such a time as this* (Esther 4:14)?

God may have brought you where He wants to make use of you for the converting of thousands, but you must be converted yourself first. Christ will not use you unless you are first His own. You must yield yourself up to Him and be saved by His precious blood; then, after that, come and give to Him all the little talent that you may have. Ask Him to make as much use of you as He did of the boy with the five barley loaves.

Chapter 19

Our Meager Loaves
in Christ's Hands

He blessed and broke and gave the loaves to his
disciples, and the disciples to the multitude.
(Matthew 14:19)

Now we see that those loaves do not so much suggest the
thought of the boy's sacrifice as of the Savior's power.
Is it not a wonderful thing that Christ, the living God, would
associate Himself with our feebleness, our lack of talent, our
ignorance, and our little faith? Yet He does so. If we are not
associated with Him, we can do nothing; but when we come
into living contact with Him, we can do all things. Those barley loaves in Christ's hands become full of food for the entire
crowd. Out of His hands they are nothing but barley cakes;
in His hands, associated with Him, they are in contact with
omnipotence.

You who love the Lord Jesus Christ, have you thought of
this – of bringing all that you possess to Him so that it will be
linked with Him? That brain of yours can be associated with
the teachings of His Spirit. That heart of yours can be warmed

with the love of God. That tongue of yours can be touched with the live coal from off the altar (Isaiah 6:6-7). That manhood of yours can be perfectly consecrated by association with Christ.

Hear the tender command of the Lord, *Bring them here to me* (Matthew 14:18), and your whole life will be transformed. I do not say that everyone of average ability can rise to great ability by being associated with Christ through faith, but I do say that his ordinary ability, in association with Christ, will become sufficient for the occasion to which God in providence has called him.

> Do not stay behind and count your deficiencies; bring what you have and let all that you are – body, soul, and spirit – be associated with Christ.

I know that you have been praying and saying, "I don't have this," and "I cannot do that." Do not stay behind and count your deficiencies; bring what you have and let all that you are – body, soul, and spirit – be associated with Christ. Although He may not give you new abilities, the abilities you have will have new power, for they will come into a new standing toward Him. What may not be hoped for by a connection with such wisdom and might?

They were transferred to Christ. A moment ago they belonged to this boy, but now they belong to Christ. *Jesus took the loaves* (John 6:11). He has taken possession of them; they are His. Oh, Christian people, do you mean what you say when you declare that you have given yourself to Christ? If you have made a full surrender, then in that surrender will lie great power for usefulness. But do not people often say, "What if I keep a little portion back? *What means then this bleating of the sheep in my ears and the lowing of the oxen which I hear?* (1 Samuel 15:14). What about that extra thousand that you put in the stock market the other day? What about the money you have saved for more clothes you don't need?

Oh, that we had more real placing our loaves into Christ's hands! The time that you have not used for self, but given to Christ; the knowledge that you have not stored, as in a reservoir, but given to Christ; the ability that you have not used for the world, but submitted to Christ; your influence and position, your money and home, all put into Christ's hands and considered not to be your own, but to be His from this time on – this is the way in which the needs of the downtrodden will be met and the world's hunger will be satisfied. However, we are astonished at the very outset by the lack of this complete dedication of everything to Christ.

As these loaves were given to Jesus, so they were accepted by Jesus. They were not only dedicated, but they were also consecrated. Jesus took the five barley loaves and the two little fish, and in doing so He seemed to say, "These will be sufficient for Me." As the Revised Version has it, *Jesus therefore took the loaves.* Was there any reason why He should? Yes, because they were brought to Him. They were willingly presented to Him. There was a need of them, and He could use them. *Therefore* He took the loaves.

Children of God, if Christ Jesus has ever made use of you, you have often stood and wondered how the Lord could ever accept you; but there was a *therefore* in it. He saw that you were willing to win souls. He saw that the souls needed winning, and He used you, even you. Am I not now speaking to some who might be of great service if they yielded themselves unto Christ, and Christ accepted them and they became accepted in the Beloved? *To the praise of the glory of his grace, in which he has made us accepted in the beloved* (Ephesians 1:6). There were only five little barley loaves, but Jesus accepted them. There were only two small fish, brought by a little boy, but the great Christ accepted them and they became His own.

These loaves and fish were blessed by Christ as He lifted

up His eyes and gave thanks to the Father for them. Think of it. For five little loaves and two little fish, Jesus gave thanks to the Father. This was apparently a small cause for praise, but Jesus knew what He could make of them, and therefore He gave thanks for what they would soon accomplish.

"God loves us," says Augustine,[20] "for what we are becoming." Christ gave thanks for these little things because He saw what they would become. Do you not think that, having thanked the Father, He also thanked the boy? In later years, these words of gratitude would be more than enough recompense for such a tiny deed. Like the woman who cast in the two mites to the treasury (Mark 12:41-44), he gave his all, and doubtless was commended for the gift.

Though exalted in glory today, Christ is still grateful when such offerings are made to Him. He still thanks His Father when, with timid, trembling hands, we offer to Him our best, our all, however small. His heart is still made glad when we bring to Him our meager supply that it may be touched by His dear hand and blessed by His gracious lips. He loves us, not for what we are, but for what He will make us. He blesses our offerings, not for their worth, but because His power will make them worthy of His praise.

May the Lord thus bless every talent that you have! May He bless your memory. May He bless your understanding. May He bless your voices. May He bless your hearts. May He bless your minds. May He bless you all unceasingly! When He puts a blessing into the little gift and into the little grace that we have, good work begins and goes on to perfection.

After the loaves had been blessed, they were increased by Christ. Peter takes one, begins to break it, and as he breaks it, he always has as much in his hand as he started with. "Here,

---

20   Augustine (AD 354-430) was a church father, author, theologian, and bishop of Hippo in Algeria.

take a bit of fish, friend," he says. He gives a whole fish to that man, but he has a whole fish left. So he gives it to another, and another, and another, and goes on scattering the bread and scattering the fish everywhere, as quickly as he can. When he is done, he has his hands just as full of fish and as full of bread as ever.

If you serve God, you will never run dry. He who gives you something to say one Sunday will give you something to say another Sunday. Some very educated brothers are like the great wine cask of Heidelberg – they can hold so much wine that there is enough to swim in, but they put in a tap somewhere up at the top, and you never get much out. Mine is a very small barrel indeed, but the tap is down as low as it can be. You can get more out of a small tub, if you empty it, than you can out of a big one if you are only permitted to draw a little from the top.

This boy gave all his loaves and all his fish. It was not much, really, but Christ multiplied it. Be like that boy and give your all. Do not think of keeping some back for another occasion. If you are a preacher, do not think of what you will preach about the next time; think of what you are going to preach about now. It is always quite enough to get one sermon at a time. You do not need to have a stockpile, because if you get a lot stored away somewhere, there will be a stale odor about them. Even the manna that came down from heaven bred worms and smelled bad; so will your best sermons, even if the message is given by God. If it does not come down from heaven, but from your own brain, it will go bad still more quickly. Tell the people about Christ. Lead them to Jesus, and do not concern yourself about what you will say next time. Wait until next time comes, *for it shall be given you in that same hour what ye shall speak* (Matthew 10:19).

Christ's additions mean subtraction, and Christ's subtractions mean addition. He gives so that we can give away. He multiplied as soon as the disciples began to distribute, and when the distribution ended, the multiplication ended. Oh, for the grace to go on distributing! If you have received the truth from Christ, tell it to others! God will whisper it in your ear and teach you His Word, but if you stop telling it to others, if you stop trying to bless others with God's truth, it may be that God will no longer bless you or allow you to grow near to Him in communion with Him.

Putting all this together, if we all would bring our loaves and fish to the Lord Jesus Christ, He would take them and make them wholly His own. Then, when He could have simply blessed them, He will multiply them and tell us to distribute them. We could meet the needs of our own towns and the needs of the whole world down to the last person.

A Christ who can feed five thousand can feed five million. There is no limit. When once you get a miracle, you may as well have a great one. Whenever I find the critics trying to diminish miracles, it always seems to me very poor work. If it is a miracle, it is a miracle, and if you are in for a penny, you may as well be in for a dollar. If you can believe that Christ can feed fifty, then you can believe that He can feed five hundred, five thousand, five million, or five hundred million, if He wants to.

A great deal of misery was removed by this boy's basket of barley cakes. Those poor people were famished. They had been with Christ all day and had nothing to eat. If they would have been dispersed as they were, tired and hungry, many of them would have fainted or perhaps even died along the way. Oh, what would we give if we might alleviate the misery of this world! I remember the Earl of Shaftesbury saying, "I would like to live longer. I cannot bear to go out of the world while there is so much misery in it." That dear saint of God had given himself to look after the poor, the helpless, and the needy all his days.

Maybe I speak to some who never yet woke up to the idea

that if they were to bring their little all to Christ, He could make use of it in alleviating the misery of many wounded consciences who could avoid that awful misery that will come upon people if they die unforgiven and stand before the judgment seat of God without a Savior.

Yes, young man, God can make you the spiritual father of many. As I look back upon my own history, little did I dream when I first opened my mouth for Christ, in a very humble way, that I would have the honor of bringing thousands to Jesus. Blessed, blessed be His name! He has the glory of it. But I cannot help thinking that there must be some other young man – such a one as I was – whom He may call by His grace to do service for Him.

When I had a letter sent to me by the deacons of the church at New Park Street asking me to come up to London to preach, I sent it back, telling them that they had made a mistake, that I was a boy of nineteen years of age, happy among a very poor and lowly people in Cambridgeshire, who loved me, and that I could not imagine that they meant that I was to preach in London. But they returned the letter to me, saying that they knew all about it and that I must come. Ah, what a story it has been since then of the goodness and loving kindness of the Lord!

> It still pleases God, by the lowly things and things that are not, to bring to naught the things that are.

You must not think that God picks out all the very best and particularly exceptional people. It is not that way in the Bible. Some of those whom He took were very rough people; even the first apostles were mostly fishermen. Paul was an educated man, but he was like a lot of people on the list – one *born out of due time* (1 Corinthians 15:8). The rest of them were not so, but God used them, too. It still pleases God, by the lowly things and things that are not, to bring to naught the things that are.

For ye see your calling, brethren, how that not many wise men after the flesh, not many mighty, not many noble, are called: But God hath chosen the foolish things of the world to confound the wise; and God hath chosen the weak things of the world to confound the things which are mighty; And base things of the world, and things which are despised, hath God chosen, yea, and things which are not, to bring to nought things that are: That no flesh should glory in his presence. (1 Corinthians 1:26-29)

I do not want you to think highly of yourself; you only have five loaves, and they are barley – and poor barley at that. Your fish are very small, and there are only two of them. I do not want you to think much of them, but think much of Christ. Believe that, whoever you may be, if He thought it worth His while to buy you with His blood and is willing to make some use of you, it is surely worth your while to come and bring yourself and all that you have to Him who is graciously ready to accept you. Put everything into His hands and let it be said of you, *And Jesus took the loaves.* It is a part of the history of the loaves that they relieved a great deal of misery.

Jesus was glorified, for the people said that He was a prophet. *Then those men, when they had seen the miracle that Jesus did, said, This is of a truth that prophet that should come into the world* (John 6:14). The miracle of the loaves carried them back to the wilderness and to the miracle of the manna. They remembered that Moses had said, *The Lord thy God will raise up unto thee a Prophet from the midst of thee, of thy brethren, like unto me* (Deuteronomy 18:15). They longed for this Deliverer, and as the bread increased, so did their wonder, until in the multiplying loaves they saw the finger of God. *This is of a truth that prophet that should come into the world.*

That little boy, by his loaves and fish, became the revealer of Christ to the entire multitude. Who can tell, if you give your loaves to Christ, whether thousands will recognize Him as the Savior because of it? Christ is still known in the breaking of bread.

When the feast was finished, there were fragments to be gathered. This is a part of the history of the loaves – they were not lost. They were eaten, but they were still there. People were filled with them, yet there were more remaining than when the feast began. Each disciple had a basketful to carry back to his Master's feet.

Give yourself to Christ, and when you have used yourself for His glory, you will be more able to serve Him than you are now. You will find your little supply growing as you spend it. Remember John Bunyan's picture in *Pilgrim's Progress* of the man who had a roll of cloth. He unrolled it and cut off some for the poor. Then he unrolled it and cut off some more. The

> The more you do, the more you can do, by the grace of the ever-blessed One!

more he cut it, the longer it grew. John Bunyan wrote, "There was a man, and some did count him mad; The more he gave away, the more he had."

It is certainly so with talent and ability, and also with grace in the heart. The more you use it, the more there is of it. It is often so with gold and silver: the wealth of the generous person increases, while the miser grows poor. We have an old proverb that is true and is worthy of thought: "Drawn wells have the sweetest waters." If you keep continually drawing on your mind in Christ, your thoughts will get sweeter. If you continue to draw on Christ, who is your strength, your strength will get to be mightier through God. The more you do, the more you can do, by the grace of the ever-blessed One!

These loaves were written about. There are many loaves that have gone to a king's table and yet never had their story told, but this boy's five cakes and two little fish got into the Bible. If you look, you will find the barley cakes in Matthew, in Mark, in Luke, and in John. To make quite sure that we would never forget how much God can do with little things, this story is told four times, and it is the only one of Christ's miracles that has such an abundant record.

Let us put it to the test. You young people who have recently become followers of Jesus, do not take too long before you try to do something for Christ. You who have been trusting Christ for a long time and have never yet begun to work, get up and attempt some service for His sake. Aged friends and sick friends can still find something to do. Perhaps in the end we will find out that the people whom we might have excused on account of illness or weakness or poverty are the people who have done the most. That, at least, is my observation. I find that, if there is really good work done, it is usually done by someone not able to get out or by someone who very rightfully could have said, "Please excuse me from this."

How is it that so many able-bodied and gifted Christians seem to be so reluctant in the Master's service? If there is a political meeting, something about liberals and conservatives, how eager you are! You are all there, every bit of you, regarding politics, which are not worth a penny a year; but when it comes to souls being saved, many of you are as mute as fish. You go all year long without caring even for the spiritual welfare of a little child.

One of our friends gave a good answer to a brother who said to him, "I have been a member of a church now for forty years. I am a father in Israel." He asked him, "How many children do you have? How many have you brought to Christ?"

"Well," the man said, "I do not know that I ever brought anybody to Christ." Upon which our friend replied, "You call yourself a father in Israel, and yet you have no children! I think you had better wait until you have earned the title."

So do I. It would be better that we had no professors of

Christianity of that kind, but that all disciples of the Lord Jesus Christ, even though they would be much fewer in number, would be men and women who are constantly bringing forth fruit unto God in the conversion of others.

May the Lord set you all to work with this purpose!

Charles H. Spurgeon – A Brief Biography

Charles Haddon Spurgeon was born on June 19, 1834, in Kelvedon, Essex, England. He was one of seventeen children in his family (nine of whom died in infancy). His father and grandfather were Nonconformist ministers in England. Due to economic difficulties, eighteen-month-old Charles was sent to live with his grandfather, who helped teach Charles the ways of God. Later in life, Charles remembered looking at the pictures in Pilgrim's Progress and in Foxe's Book of Martyrs as a young boy.

Charles did not have much of a formal education and never went to college. He read much throughout his life though, especially books by Puritan authors.

Even with godly parents and grandparents, young Charles resisted giving in to God. It was not until he was fifteen years old that he was born again. He was on his way to his usual church, but when a heavy snowstorm prevented him from getting there, he turned in at a little Primitive Methodist chapel. Though there were only about fifteen people in attendance, the preacher spoke from Isaiah 45:22: *Look unto me, and be ye saved, all the ends of the earth.* Charles Spurgeon's eyes were opened and the Lord converted his soul.

He began attending a Baptist church and teaching Sunday school. He soon preached his first sermon, and then when he was sixteen years old, he became the pastor of a small Baptist church in Cambridge. The church soon grew to over four hundred people, and Charles Spurgeon, at the age of nineteen, moved on to become the pastor of the New Park Street Church in London. The church grew from a few hundred attenders to a few thousand. They built an addition to the church, but still needed more room to accommodate the congregation. The Metropolitan Tabernacle was built in London in 1861, seating more than 5,000 people. Pastor Spurgeon preached the simple message of the cross, and thereby attracted many people who wanted to hear God's Word preached in the power of the Holy Spirit.

On January 9, 1856, Charles married Susannah Thompson. They had twin boys, Charles and Thomas. Charles and Susannah loved each other deeply, even amidst the difficulties and troubles that they faced in life, including health problems. They helped each other spiritually, and often together read the writings of Jonathan Edwards, Richard Baxter, and other Puritan writers.

Charles Spurgeon was a friend of all Christians, but he stood firmly on the Scriptures, and it didn't please all who heard him. Spurgeon believed in and preached on the sovereignty of God, heaven and hell, repentance, revival, holiness, salvation through Jesus Christ alone, and the infallibility and necessity of the Word of God. He spoke against worldliness and hypocrisy among Christians, and against Roman Catholicism, ritualism, and modernism.

One of the biggest controversies in his life was known as the "Down-Grade Controversy." Charles Spurgeon believed that some pastors of his time were "down-grading" the faith by compromising with the world or the new ideas of the age. He said that some pastors were denying the inspiration of the

Bible, salvation by faith alone, and the truth of the Bible in other areas, such as creation. Many pastors who believed what Spurgeon condemned were not happy about this, and Spurgeon eventually resigned from the Baptist Union.

Despite some difficulties, Spurgeon became known as the "Prince of Preachers." He opposed slavery, started a pastors' college, opened an orphanage, led in helping feed and clothe the poor, had a book fund for pastors who could not afford books, and more.

Charles Spurgeon remains one of the most published preachers in history. His sermons were printed each week (even in the newspapers), and then the sermons for the year were re-issued as a book at the end of the year. The first six volumes, from 1855-1860, are known as *The Park Street Pulpit*, while the next fifty-seven volumes, from 1861-1917 (his sermons continued to be published long after his death), are known as *The Metropolitan Tabernacle Pulpit*. He also oversaw a monthly magazine-type publication called *The Sword and the Trowel,* and Spurgeon wrote many books, including *Lectures to My Students, All of Grace, Around the Wicket Gate, Advice for Seekers, John Ploughman's Talks, The Soul Winner, Words of Counsel for Christian Workers, Cheque Book of the Bank of Faith, Morning and Evening,* his autobiography, and more, including some commentaries, such as his twenty-year study on the Psalms – *The Treasury of David.*

Charles Spurgeon often preached ten times a week, preaching to an estimated ten million people during his lifetime. He usually preached from only one page of notes, and often from just an outline. He read about six books each week. During his lifetime, he had read *The Pilgrim's Progress* through more than one hundred times. When he died, his personal library consisted of more than 12,000 books. However, the Bible always remained the most important book to him.

Spurgeon was able to do what he did in the power of God's

Holy Spirit because he followed his own advice – he met with God every morning before meeting with others, and he continued in communion with God throughout the day.

Charles Spurgeon suffered from gout, rheumatism, and some depression, among other health problems. He often went to Menton, France, to recuperate and rest. He preached his final sermon at the Metropolitan Tabernacle on June 7, 1891, and died in France on January 31, 1892, at the age of fifty-seven. He was buried in Norwood Cemetery in London.

Charles Haddon Spurgeon lived a life devoted to God. His sermons and writings continue to influence Christians all over the world.

Other Updated Spurgeon Titles

Words of Warning, by Charles H. Spurgeon

This book, *Words of Warning*, is an analysis of people and the gospel of Christ. Under inspiration of the Holy Spirit, Charles H. Spurgeon sheds light on the many ways people may refuse to come to Christ, but he also shines a brilliant light on how we can be saved. Unsaved or wavering individuals will be convicted, and if they allow it, they will be led to Christ. Sincere Christians will be happy and blessed as they consider the great salvation with which they have been saved.

Available where books are sold.

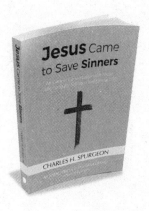

Jesus Came to Save Sinners,
by Charles H. Spurgeon

This is a heart-level conversation with you, the reader. Every excuse, reason, and roadblock for not coming to Christ is examined and duly dealt with. If you think you may be too bad, or if perhaps you really are bad and you sin either openly or behind closed doors, you will discover that life in Christ is for you too. You can reject the message of salvation by faith, or you can choose to live a life of sin after professing faith in Christ, but you cannot change the truth as it is, either for yourself or for others. As such, it behooves you and your family to embrace truth, claim it for your own, and be genuinely set free for now and eternity. Come and embrace this free gift of God, and live a victorious life for Him.

Available where books are sold.

According to Promise, by Charles H. Spurgeon

The first part of this book is meant to be a sieve to separate the chaff from the wheat. Use it on your own soul. It may be the most profitable and beneficial work you have ever done. He who looked into his accounts and found that his business was losing money was saved from bankruptcy. This may happen also to you. If, however, you discover that your heavenly business is prospering, it will be a great comfort to you. You cannot lose by honestly searching your own heart.

The second part of this book examines God's promises to His children. The promises of God not only exceed all precedent, but they also exceed all imitation. No one has been able to compete with God in the language of liberality. The promises of God are as much above all other promises as the heavens are above the earth.

Available where books are sold.

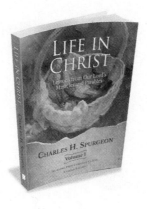

Life in Christ (Vol. 1), **by Charles H. Spurgeon**

Men who were led by the hand or groped their way along the wall to reach Jesus were touched by his finger and went home without a guide, rejoicing that Jesus Christ had opened their eyes. Jesus is still able to perform such miracles. And, with the power of the Holy Spirit, his Word will be expounded and we'll watch for the signs to follow, expecting to see them at once. Why shouldn't those who read this be blessed with the light of heaven? This is my heart's inmost desire.

I can't put fine words together. I've never studied speech. In fact, my heart loathes the very thought of intentionally speaking with fine words when souls are in danger of eternal separation from God. No, I work to speak straight to your hearts and consciences, and if there is anyone with faith to receive, God will bless them with fresh revelation.

– Charles H. Spurgeon

Available where books are sold.

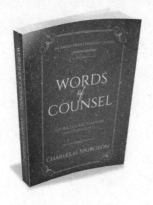

Words of Counsel, by Charles H. Spurgeon

Is there any occupation as profitable or rewarding as that of winning souls for Christ? It is a desirable employment, and the threshold for entry into this profession is set at a level any Christian may achieve – you must only love the Lord God with all your heart, soul, and mind; and your fellow man as yourself. This work is for all genuine Christians, of all walks of life. This is for you, fellow Christian.

Be prepared to be inspired, challenged, and convicted. Be prepared to weep, for the Holy Spirit may touch you deeply as you consider your coworkers, your neighbors, the children you know, and how much the Lord cares for these individuals. But you will also be equipped. Charles Spurgeon knew something about winning souls, and he holds nothing back as he shares biblical wisdom and practical application regarding the incredible work the Lord wants to do through His people to reach the lost.

Available where books are sold.

The *Soul Winner,* by Charles H. Spurgeon

As an individual, you may ask, How can I, an average person, do anything to reach the lost? Or if a pastor, you may be discouraged and feel ineffective with your congregation, much less the world. Or perhaps you don't yet have a heart for the lost. Whatever your excuse, it's time to change. Overcome yourself and learn to make a difference in your church and the world around you. It's time to become an effective soul winner for Christ.

As Christians, our main business is to win souls. But, in Spurgeon's own words, "like shoeing-smiths, we need to know a great many things. Just as the smith must know about horses and how to make shoes for them, so we must know about souls and how to win them for Christ." Learn about souls, and how to win them, from one of the most acclaimed soul winners of all time.

Available where books are sold.

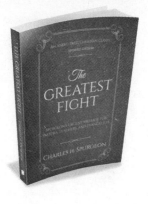

The Greatest Fight, by Charles H. Spurgeon

This book examines three things that are of utmost importance in this fight of faith. The first is *our armory*, which is the inspired Word of God. The second is *our army*, the church of the living God, which we must lead under our Lord's command. The third is *our strength*, by which we wear the armor and use the sword.

The message in this book, when originally presented by Charles Spurgeon in his final address to his own Pastor's College, was received rapturously and enthusiastically. It was almost immediately published and distributed around the world and in several languages. After Charles Spurgeon's death in 1892, 34,000 copies were printed and distributed to pastors and leaders in England through Mrs. Spurgeon's book fund. It is with great pleasure that we present this updated and very relevant book to the Lord's army of today.

Available where books are sold.